SUPERMAN:
THE MOVIE

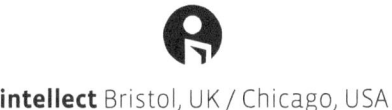

intellect Bristol, UK / Chicago, USA

First published in the UK in 2018 by
Intellect, The Mill, Parnall Road, Fishponds, Bristol, BS16 3JG, UK

First published in the USA in 2018 by
Intellect, The University of Chicago Press, 1427 E. 60th Street, Chicago, IL 60637, USA

Copyright © 2018 Intellect Ltd

All rights reserved. No part of this publication may be reproduced, stored in a retrieval system or transmitted, in any form or by any means, electronic, mechanical, photocopying, recording or otherwise, without written permission.

Superman and all related indicia are trademarks of DC Comics, Inc. This book is not sponsored, approved or authorized by DC Comics, Inc.

A catalogue record for this book is available from the British Library.

Copy-editing: MPS Technology
Cover Design: Aleksandra Szumlas
Layout Design and Typesetting: Holly Rose
Production Manager: Faith Newcombe

ISBN: 978-1-78320-959-0
ePDF: 978-1-78320-961-3
ePUB: 978-1-78320-960-6

SUPERMAN:
THE MOVIE –
THE 40TH ANNIVERSARY INTERVIEWS

by Gary Bettinson

intellect Bristol, UK / Chicago, USA

CONTENTS

07
ACKNOWLEDGEMENTS

09
INTRODUCTION
Superman: The Movie at 40

18
THE INTERVIEWS

18
PIERRE SPENGLER
PRODUCER

28
ILYA SALKIND
EXECUTIVE PRODUCER

40
RICHARD DONNER
DIRECTOR

52
MARGOT KIDDER
LOIS LANE

84
MARC MCCLURE
JIMMY OLSEN

94
JEFF EAST
YOUNG CLARK KENT

104
SARAH DOUGLAS
URSA

118
JACK O'HALLORAN
NON

127
NOTES

131
REFERENCES

133
FILMS CITED

ACKNOWLEDGEMENTS

This book is dedicated to the memory of Margot Kidder, who died on 13 May 2018.

Special thanks to the participants in this book: Richard Donner, Sarah Douglas, Jeff East, Margot Kidder, Marc McClure, Jack O'Halloran, Ilya Salkind and Pierre Spengler. I am also grateful to Dean Cain, Derek Maki, Lee Pfeiffer and Dave Worrall.

I am especially indebted to Tim Mitchell, Faith Newcombe, Aleksandra Szumlas, May Yao and Jessica Lovett at Intellect.

Thanks, as ever, to Shirley, Robert, Paul and Lucie.

INTRODUCTION
SUPERMAN:
THE MOVIE AT 40

Now in its 40th anniversary year, *Superman: The Movie* (1978) has soared to staggering heights of popularity and prestige. In 2017, it was inducted into the National Film Register, recognized for its 'cultural, historic, and aesthetic importance' (Itzkoff 2017). In the same year, Warner Brothers issued an expanded edition of *Superman* on Blu-ray, an item greeted fervently by fans; director Richard Donner was feted by the Academy of Motion Picture Arts and Sciences; and two tentpole pictures – *Wonder Woman* and *Justice League* – affectionately quoted *Superman*'s scenes and iconography. Few films of this vintage demonstrate a comparable hold on contemporary culture. Forty years on, *Superman* remains a fixture on network television, youths wear apparel exhorting others to 'Kneel', and contemporary auteurs – from Christopher Nolan to Bryan Singer – acknowledge the film as a seminal influence. A cultural event in its day, *Superman* has become a touchstone of popular cinema at its most dynamic and exhilarating.

The making of *Superman* was no less compelling, as the interviewees in this book testify. From the outset, the production was steeped in controversy. Critics castigated the project on the grounds of excess: a mammoth production budget that would swell to unprecedented proportions; astronomical salaries granted to its headline stars; and the sheer hubris displayed by the film's producers for mounting not one but two Superman movies, to be filmed concurrently rather than back-to-back. Throughout shooting, too, *Superman* acquired the aura of calamity, the production plagued by turmoil. Rumours abounded of bickering lead actors and screenwriters vying for credit. Release dates came and went. Even after the film's theatrical release, the backstage strife rumbled on. An apparently irreparable feud between the director and the producers caught headlines. Lawsuits filed by the principal players provided further grist for the mill, fuelling the notion that *Superman* was a project propelled by avarice. Most films would be cast into shadow by such off-screen intrigue. That *Superman* transcends its fraught production history is testament both to its inherent quality and to the artistic contributions of its creators.

The participants in this book – director Richard Donner, producers Ilya Salkind and Pierre Spengler, and actors Margot Kidder, Marc McClure, Jeff East, Sarah Douglas and Jack O'Halloran – recount and reflect upon *Superman*'s turbulent production in detail and with remarkable candour.[1] Still, the interviews go beyond the sensationalistic: they provide rare insights into the day-to-day realities of blockbuster film-making – a high-concept mode of production still in its infancy in the late 1970s. Collectively, the

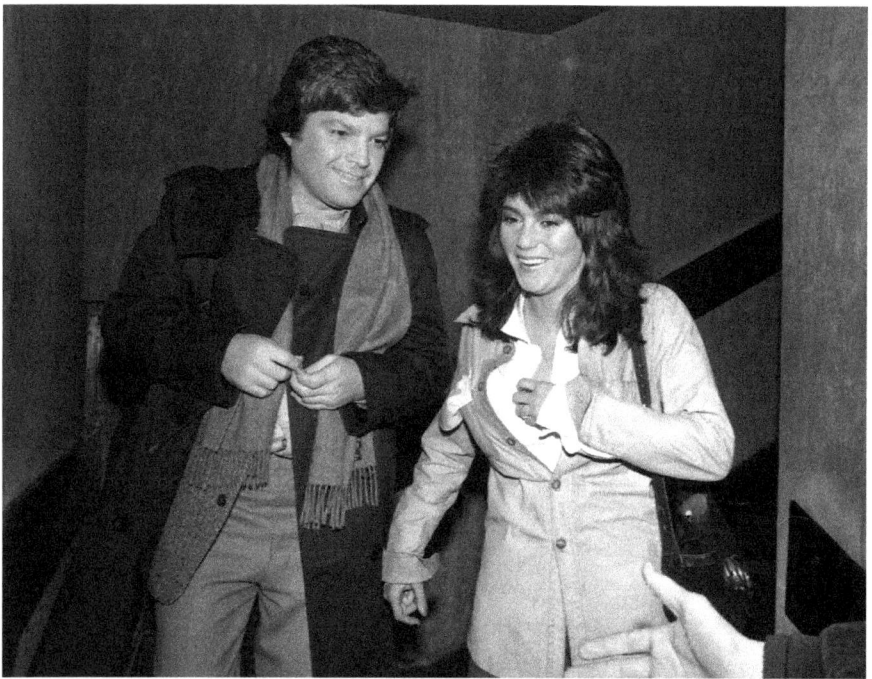

Figure 1: *Superman: The Movie* was the brainchild of European film producer, Ilya Salkind (left).

interviews furnish an oral history not only of the making of *Superman* (and its immediate sequel), but also of big-budget film production in the New Hollywood era.

Conceived by European producers Alexander Salkind, Ilya Salkind and Pierre Spengler, the Superman 'package' blended commercialism with quality. The producers, looking for both pedigree and marketability, assembled a distinguished cadre of collaborators: Mario Puzo, a recent Oscar winner for *The Godfather* (1972), wrote the *Superman* screenplay; David Newman and Robert Benton, esteemed writers of *Bonnie and Clyde* (1967), furnished additional drafts, along with Leslie Newman;[2] John Barry, feted for his work on *Star Wars* (1977), came on board as production designer; Geoffrey Unsworth, an Oscar recipient for *Cabaret* (1972), took up the role of lighting cameraman; and John Williams, fresh from a trio of Oscar victories for *Fiddler on the Roof* (1971), *Jaws* (1975) and *Star Wars*, signed on as musical composer. The high-profile casting of Marlon Brando and Gene Hackman, both recently bestowed Best Actor awards, conferred further credibility upon the production.[3] Belying its comic-book material, *Superman* was packaged as much as a prestige picture as a high-end blockbuster.

Nevertheless, its blockbuster status drew scorn from certain divisions. Budgeted at $55 million, the two-film package provoked charges of profligacy, excess and obscenity. That Brando would be paid $3.7 million for twelve days of shooting – an outrageous transaction in 1978 – did nothing to assuage the project's detractors.[4] Still, the Salkinds trusted their own business acumen. As producers of *The Three Musketeers* (1973) and *The Four Musketeers* (1974), they knew the economic benefits of a two-picture package. As for Brando, his casting proved decisive in attracting the film's other major players, many of whom sought screen time – or simply screen credit – with the revered Method actor. Suddenly, an impressive roster of talent coalesced: Harry Andrews (2nd Elder), Ned Beatty (Otis), Jackie Cooper (Perry White), Sarah Douglas (Ursa), Jeff East (Young Clark Kent), Glenn Ford (Pa Kent), Gene Hackman (Lex Luthor), Trevor Howard (1st Elder), Margot Kidder (Lois Lane), Marc McClure (Jimmy Olsen), Jack O'Halloran (Non), Valerie Perrine (Eve Teschmacher), Maria Schell (Vond-Ah), Terence Stamp (General Zod), Phyllis Thaxter (Ma Kent) and Susannah York (Lara). Cameo roles were afforded to Kirk Alyn and Noel Neill, veterans of earlier renderings of the Superman legend.[5]

More elusive was the actor destined to play Superman and Clark Kent. A litany of marquee stars circled the role, until – at the behest of casting agent, Lynn Stalmaster – the producers granted an audition to newcomer Christopher Reeve. The actor had scant film experience: his sole movie appearance, in submarine drama *Gray Lady Down* (1978), amounted to little more than a walk-on part. But his understated characterization of Superman – sincere, chivalrous, innately virtuous – set him above the competition. 'I tried to downplay being a hero and emphasize being a friend', Reeve would later write, identifying here what he felt to be 'the key to the part'. As for Clark Kent, he 'based the character [...] on the young Cary Grant' (Reeve 1999: 197).

Before discovering Reeve, however, the Salkinds had negotiated a string of upheavals. Plans to shoot *Superman* in Rome had to be aborted once the producers hired Brando, whose participation in the 'obscene' *Last Tango in Paris* (1972) put him at the mercy of the Italian authorities. Subsequently, the Salkinds relocated the Superman production to England. This forced them to sever ties with Guy Hamilton, the director assigned to direct *Superman* and *Superman II* – as a virtual tax exile, Hamilton was prohibited from working extensively in England. From one angle, Hamilton had been a judicious appointment: having spent a decade directing James Bond movies, he had tried-and-tested expertise in the action-adventure genre. From another angle, however, Hamilton's fondness for comedy, while germane to the Bond franchise, conformed less well to the Superman material. His departure from *Superman* cast the production adrift: the screenplay now bore Hamilton's fingerprints, dappled with parodic humour; and reels of flying tests, developed under Hamilton's aegis, yielded imperfect simulations of a man in flight. The production in limbo, the Salkinds had reached crisis point: faced with an unsatisfactory script, inadequate special effects, a lead role impossible to fill, dwindling coffers and a looming start date, they wrestled to control a rudderless behemoth.

Into this milieu came Richard Donner. Fresh from acclaimed blockbuster *The Omen* (1976), the director ideally fulfilled the Salkinds' recruitment criteria: critical respectability and commercial success. He was hired. Almost immediately, Donner reshaped Hamilton's overarching approach to the material, rejecting comedy in favour of 'verisimilitude' – a term that would summarize the film's conceptual framework. Now, all efforts were geared towards finding truthfulness within the story's fantastic premise. 'The story had to have a sense of reality', Donner told me, 'and the reality had to be portrayed by the characters and brought to life in their relationships. *Superman* needed to have reality, instead of farce – which is what the original script was' (Bettinson 2018). To this end, Donner hired writer Tom Mankiewicz to purge the script's parodic elements, enliven the protagonists' romance and anchor the action to the realm of believability. So central was the concept of verisimilitude to *Superman*'s overall aesthetic that it ultimately inspired the film's marketing hook: 'You'll believe a man can fly'.

It also prompted Donner to hire Christopher Reeve, whose approach to the character dovetailed with his own. '[Donner] respected my desire to make the character as human and natural as possible', Reeve later claimed (Reeve 1999: 198). With the title role finally cast, Donner presided over principal photography of *Superman: The Movie* on 24 March 1977. The bloated shooting schedule, which stretched until October 1977 and encompassed location filming in Canada and the United States, sparked enmity between Donner and the producers. Donner pursued perfection, but his methods seemed protracted and profligate. The Salkinds demanded expediency. Donner regarded the producers as philistines, prepared to sacrifice art for commerce. As relationships curdled, the Salkinds enlisted director Richard Lester – their efficient collaborator on the Musketeers series – to serve as de facto middleman and adviser to Donner.

Shooting *Superman* and its sequel together proved untenable, and the Salkinds chose to postpone the completion of *Superman II*, even though Donner had filmed many of its key scenes. Instead, effort was channelled into finishing the first instalment. After a year spent in post-production, *Superman: The Movie* opened across America on 18 December 1978, becoming the highest-grossing film of the late 1970s. Just as audiences embraced the film, so too did critics. Many reviewers hailed Reeve's performance as definitive. *Newsweek*, meanwhile, declared that 'Donner's shaping of the film amounts to a major feat in filmmaking' (Kroll 1979: 48). *Superman*'s appeal, as Noël Carroll has observed, rested partly in nostalgia for reassuring moral absolutes – the film recalled 'times of which it is said that good and evil were sharply etched' (Carroll 1998: 248). Arriving at the tail-end of a decade notable for its pessimistic movies, *Superman* signalled Hollywood's return to fundamentally hopeful, beatific storytelling.

The bona fide success of *Superman* justified a sequel, but Donner's public recriminations against Pierre Spengler rankled with the producers, who duly dismissed him. *Superman II* resumed filming in 1979 under the auspices of Richard Lester, now the film's official director. According to Directors Guild dictates, however, Lester would be denied credit unless he could lay claim to the majority of the sequel's footage. Thus, the incumbent director scotched several scenes shot by Donner. Lester also reworked the shooting script bearing Donner's imprimatur (and that of Mankiewicz, who abandoned the production in solidarity with Donner). *Superman II* premiered in 1980, and few observers noticed the suture marks separating Lester's footage from Donner's. Not until 2006 did viewers behold Donner's discarded scenes: *Superman II*: *The Richard Donner Cut* fused original screen-test recordings with previously unseen material, including the substantial input of Marlon Brando (a conspicuous absentee in Lester's version).

After the success of *Superman II* the Salkinds rallied again, ushering in another sequel and a spin-off entry, *Supergirl* (1984). Released in 1983, Richard Lester's *Superman III* swept the franchise off track: ratcheting its comedic scenes to the level of slapstick, the film fell prey to stunt casting and antic humour. As Reeve accurately observed, '[*Superman III*] became more a Richard Pryor comedy vehicle than a proper Superman film' (Reeve 1999: 202). Still, *Superman III* turned a profit, and at least one major set-piece – in which Clark Kent battles a Kryptonite-addled Superman in an automobile junkyard – became a fan favourite. Less memorable was Jeannot Szwarc's *Supergirl*, a wistful, strangely lethargic enterprise that fizzled at the box office. Wary of diminishing returns, the Salkinds sold the Superman movie rights. Exploitation outfit Cannon Films aimed to reinvigorate the series, but *Superman IV: The Quest for Peace* (1987) spluttered at the box office, and the franchise foundered for almost 20 years.

According to Reeve, '*Superman IV* was simply a catastrophe from start to finish. That failure was a huge blow to my career' (Reeve 1999: 228). Still, Reeve's filmography forms a distinguished body of work, no matter the critical derision afforded *Superman IV*. Several of his films represent indelible achievements: *Somewhere in Time* (1980),

Deathtrap (1982), *The Bostonians* (1984), *Street Smart* (1987) and *The Remains of the Day* (1993) – not to mention *Superman: The Movie* and *Superman II*. Even in less exalted films such as *Switching Channels* (1988) and *Noises Off...* (1992), Reeve's talent shines through. He tragically sustained a spinal-cord injury in 1995, and died in 2004, aged 52.

For all its off-screen turmoil, *Superman: The Movie* represents a landmark in Hollywood cinema. Historically, the film consolidated the 1970s blockbuster strategy, marshalling a pre-sold property (the cross-media Superman brand), bankable stars, technological innovations (the 'Zoptic' front-projection system; Dolby Stereo surround sound), mass distribution, saturation advertising and a multitude of ancillary tie-in products (from John Williams' soundtrack album to 'walking billboard' Superman T-shirts). Not least, *Superman* both inaugurated and legitimized the high-concept comic-book film, propelling the genre to artistic heights. Today, the film wields a towering influence on superhero cinema and beyond; look no further than Steven Spielberg's *Ready Player One* (2018) for evidence of *Superman*'s impact on American popular culture. Its singularity owes much to the interviewees in this book, as well as to scores of relatively unsung production personnel (some of whom are cited in these pages). Above all, debt is owed to Jerry Siegel and Joe Shuster, whose maiden Superman strip marks its 80th year in 2018. *Superman: The Movie* stands as a fitting tribute to their creation.

"There was really no example of comic-book movies before Superman. By putting the elements together as we did – a prestigious director, a prestigious writer, and so forth – we gave the film weight. Superman was practically a first."

PIERRE SPENGLER

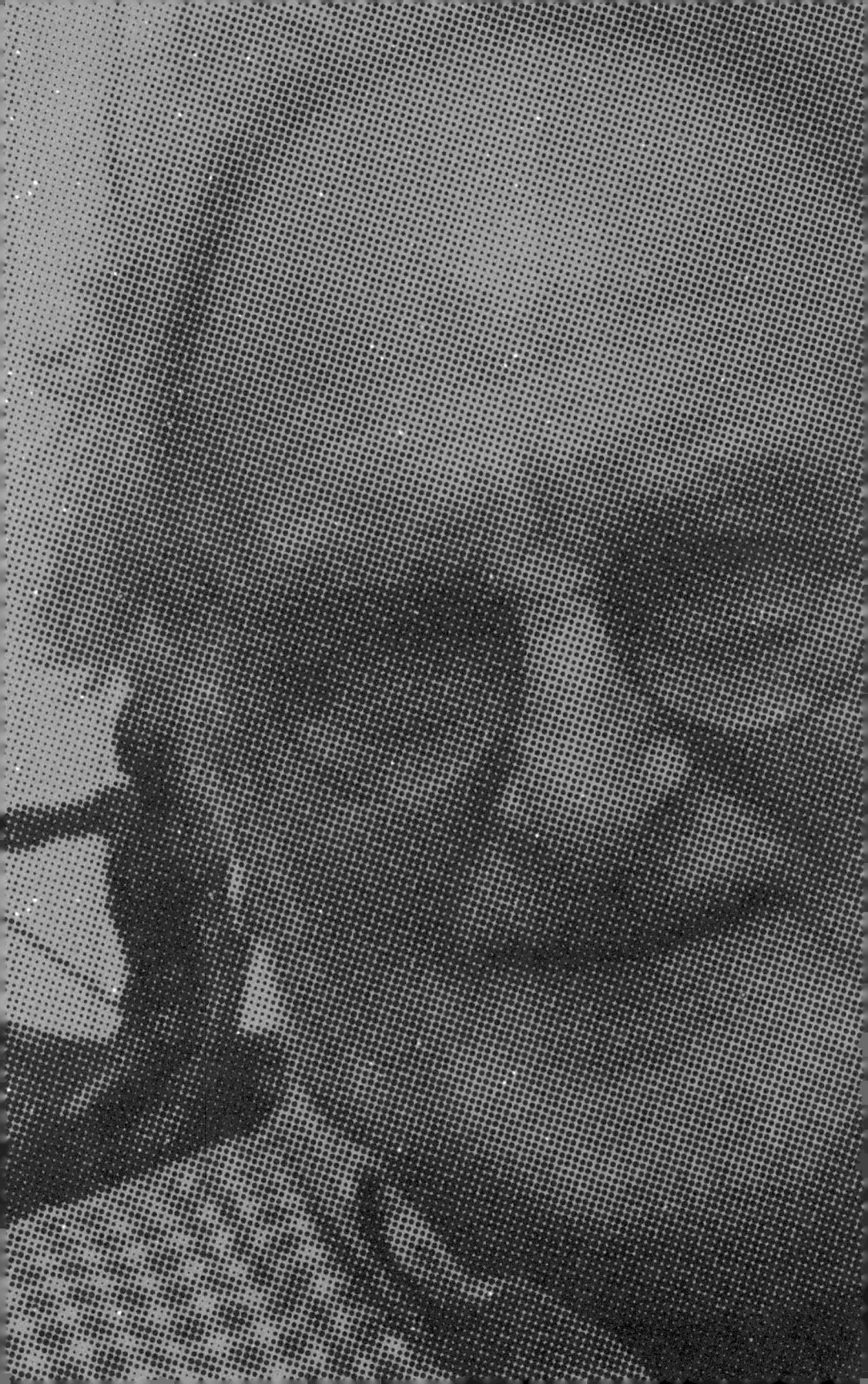

PIERRE SPENGLER
PRODUCER

Gary Bettinson: As producer, you negotiated the Superman film rights with DC Comics. Who led the negotiations on behalf of DC Comics?
Pierre Spengler: A gentleman named Bernie Kashdan. He was the vice president for business affairs. And there was also a gentleman named Carmine Infantino, who intervened on a number of occasions. He was the president of the company at that time but not very experienced in this kind of negotiation. I mean, he was a genius comic-book artist, but when we came into the complications of a film negotiation he required certain things, or demanded certain things, that were basically unacceptable to us. We almost reached a deadlock. Eventually the deal was arbitrated, as it were, by Bill Sarnoff who was president of Warner Books. He was technically higher up than Carmine. And Bill helped, because he had more experience in these kinds of negotiations.

GB: Do you remember the kinds of demands that Infantino made?
PS: Sure. The monetary terms we had agreed with Bernie Kashdan. He had run those terms by his superiors, and so all the monetary terms and everything were fine. The stumbling block was the approvals clause, where DC was so wary of what could be done with their precious characters. They wanted to have a whole set of approvals. And we did work out a set of approvals eventually, but at the beginning Carmine basically was saying: 'Well, you write a script and if we don't like it we'll tell you that we don't like it. And then you should write another one and present it to us.' [Laughs.] And we said, 'That's completely impractical – we'll be here until the cows come home. You'll just keep disapproving our script and we'll never make a movie.' So we finally worked out a mechanism whereby if they didn't approve the script they had to tell us *why* and provide suggestions on how to correct it. They couldn't just say 'No' – they had to say 'No, but if you do this...' and then we would make the corrections and present the script to DC again, and if we did follow their suggestions the script was deemed approved. But if we had some alternative suggestions, DC still had the right of approval over those. It was very, very complicated. So then we decided that we would have a series of conferences

with Carmine representing DC Comics, Mario Puzo (who was then the writer of the Superman script) and ourselves [the Salkinds and Spengler], the producers. We didn't even have a director on-board at that time. We all agreed that we would record these conferences and make live transcripts of them, and that whatever was agreed during these conferences would be deemed approved and could be incorporated into the script.

GB: So Infantino was chiefly concerned with DC's 'integrity of character' clause, which related to the character of Superman and the ways you were permitted to portray him on film?
PS: Yes, and that's what is impossible to put on the page. You can only sort of put generalities. Ultimately, we had to live with their approvals clause. DC were also supposed to approve the rushes, to make sure the rushes accorded with what was approved previously. There was a representative – who was in fact a Warner representative in London – named Paul Hitchcock, who became a representative of DC Comics and watched the rushes every day. To be honest, though, we didn't have any major conflicts with DC. We set out to make a Superman movie that was loyal to the comic-book image. We were not trying to make a spoof of the character, or anything like that.

GB: Given your fidelity to the material, did the DC executives have confidence in the project?
PS: Well, while we were negotiating the contract with DC, the DC people called Warner Brothers. Warner was DC's sister company. They called someone at Warner and said, 'Look, the producers who made *The Three Musketeers* want to buy the rights to Superman and make a movie.' And the person at Warner, who was a high-up production executive at the company, said, 'Well, take as much money upfront as you can, because Superman will never make a movie.'

GB: Were you heavily involved in the merchandising of **Superman***, or were the ancillary products principally controlled by Warner Brothers and DC Comics?*
PS: That was principally Warner. But there was a certain conflict, for want of a better word, between the DC Comics merchandising and the film merchandising. Profits from the film merchandising had to be shared with us, the producers. But profits from the DC Comics merchandising did not have to be shared with us, because that merchandise was comic-book based. Consequently, I think that Warner favoured the DC Comics merchandising rather than the film merchandising. There was some film merchandising but not much. The merchandising negotiations were done in 1974. Basically we said, 'OK, if the merchandise is only related to the character or to the comic book, then the profits belong 100 per cent to DC Comics; but if the merchandise is related to the film – if it uses actors, props, visualizations, or whatever, from the film – then we share.'

GB: I understand that DC Comics had approval over the casting of all the actors in the film. It has been widely reported that figures such as Muhammad Ali and Al Pacino were approved…
PS: Well, we put together a list which was indeed a very silly list. We had a list because, again, we said, 'We can't just go to DC and every time we come up with an actor they say they don't like him.' So we thought, 'Let's put together a list of actors to be pre-approved by DC.' We had names of famous stars to play Superman, and of course we eventually didn't use any of them. We went for Chris.

GB: Warren Beatty has stated that he was the first actor to be offered the role of Superman. Was he indeed the first actor you approached?
PS: I know we [the producers] did talk about stars. I'm trying to think if Warren was one of them. It could have been the case, because he would have been right for the role. The people that we thought of, and actually made offers to, included Paul Newman. But Warren? Possibly. He would have been good, actually.

GB: Did you insert a morality clause into the contracts of all the actors?
PS: No, not with all the actors. I think we put a clause in Chris Reeve's contract, because we foresaw the possibility of him appearing in Superman sequels. Therefore, so long as he was working for us, potentially to appear in a sequel, we indeed put a clause in his contract stating that he couldn't do a porno film. Not that he ever would have done that!

GB: So this clause didn't pertain to his roles in regular movies outside the Superman franchise?
PS: No. If memory serves me right, in between *Superman II* and *Superman III*, he did a film [*Deathtrap*] with Michael Caine where he was gay. And he played a crooked cardinal in some other movie [*Monsignor*]. So it was a broad clause. We didn't want him to do something that was, you know, porno or X-rated.

GB: During pre-production and production, you made a number of high-profile trips to the Cannes Film Festival. Was the purpose of these visits purely to promote Superman: The Movie, *or was it also to attract financiers?*
PS: When you go to Cannes, there are several reasons to do so. One of the reasons is networking, where you meet the people of the industry and basically exchange thoughts with them. The second thing is to sell your film. When we first went to Cannes, we had only Mario Puzo as a name attached to *Superman*. And so we announced the film and immediately people were sort of intrigued. They showed some interest but we didn't sign any contracts at that time. In Cannes of 1976, we announced the film with Guy Hamilton directing, Marlon Brando acting and Gene Hackman acting. And then people got crazy, because that was a really extraordinary package. Before that, people hadn't

quite imagined what *Superman* could be. Now they could somehow visualize it. And we did sell quite a lot of territories during that trip to Cannes. We sold finally the US and the UK distribution rights to Warner Brothers. And then in 1977, we came back to Cannes and we were able to show some footage from *Superman* – around ten minutes of a promo reel. We showed that to Warner and then Warner bought all the unsold territories.

GB: Do you recall which scenes were shown in the promo reel?
PS: It was mostly scenes from Krypton. That's what had been shot by then.

GB: Was Brando's contract difficult to negotiate? Was it difficult to convince him to act in a comic-book movie? Obviously **Superman: The Movie** *would go on to change the nature of that type of film...*
PS: Well, that's exactly the thing. There was really no example of comic-book movies before. None that would count, anyway. There were a couple of Superman movies that had been done, but as far as I recall they sort of spliced together some television episodes.[6] Okay, our movie was based on the comic book, but by putting the elements together as we did – you know, a prestigious director, a prestigious writer and so forth – we gave it weight. There were no comic-book movies at that time. *Superman* was practically a first.

GB: Was product placement an important source of financing for the film? A box of Cheerios features prominently in one shot in **Superman**...
PS: No, it wasn't an important part. We did have a deal with Cheerios. There's no point saying we didn't. [Laughs.] But it was a very tiny deal. And Cheerios breakfast was Americana. You know, Donner's sense of Americana was precious, because obviously we [the producers] are European and we don't have the same sense of Americana. So that's why the Cheerios box was there.

GB: Why did you decide to shoot two Superman movies simultaneously? The Musketeers films were not initially conceived as two films, whereas the Superman package from inception included two movies, isn't that so?
PS: Yeah, that's true. With *Musketeers*, we first wanted to make a big epic, but then we realized that we would lose a big audience by making a film that was too long. That's why we decided to cut it into two films. And there was a very neat point in the middle of the story to do it – when D'Artagnan becomes a musketeer. Having done that, and having seen basically that there are some economic advantages to making two movies at the same time, we decided to make the first two Superman movies at the same time. That was, as it were, the business plan. But in the end we didn't manage to do it, because the costs and schedule went so wildly over on the first Superman movie that we had to focus on finishing the first movie and then decide whether to finish the second movie or not, depending on the success of the first.

GB: Was abandoning Superman II *ever a genuine option? Regardless of the success or failure of* Superman: The Movie*, Donner had already shot a lot of footage for* Superman II.

PS: Well, not so much footage, you see. Basically, if you look at *Superman II*, the Richard Lester version, there was about 20 per cent of footage that had been shot simultaneously with *Superman: The Movie*. Most of it was Gene Hackman's footage. I think we had done the trucker scene in the diner too;[7] we'd shot that already. But that was it. So, to answer your question – well, if the first film had been a flop I think we would have just abandoned the idea of the second one. We might have made an even longer TV version of *Superman: The Movie*. We already did a long TV version of the first one.[8] So maybe we would have expanded it even more.

GB: Was Alexander Salkind a frequent visitor to the set of Superman: The Movie*? I know that he wasn't comfortable travelling by plane.*

PS: He wasn't only uncomfortable; he didn't fly at all. No, he wasn't in London all that much. Really it was my job, and his son [Ilya] was in London also. Between the two of us we would run the show. And we'd report back to Alex. Generally bad reports. [Laughs.]

GB: You worked with Christopher Reeve on three Superman films.

PS: On the three, absolutely, yes.

GB: And Superman: The Movie *made him an international film star. How did he change over the five years that you worked together?*

PS: You know, his head grew a little, which is natural. Anybody's head would grow a little in those circumstances. But look, he always was a professional, he was always there doing the job. He was always a wonderful actor and able to do the two parts. And he took it very seriously. You know, he was great. I've got nothing but praise for him.

GB: Did he take on more responsibility as the series developed?

PS: He would suggest certain things. Certain things we had to stop him from doing. On *Superman III*, he wanted to be on a crane, flying near the ground, just over the wheat fields. He wanted to do that himself, but I said, 'I'm sorry, you're not doing that!' [Laughs.] It was much too dangerous.

GB: You enlisted Richard Lester as a producer on Superman: The Movie*. Did he direct second-unit material on the film?*

PS: No. Well, he might have done one bit of filming when we were shooting the Smallville scenes in Canada. But it wasn't our intention that Lester direct any scenes in *Superman: The Movie*. The intention was really for him to help in production decisions and maybe give a bit of advice to Donner. You know, we were racking our brains to find a powerful ending for *Superman*. We had written the script for *Superman* and *Superman II*, and we did not have a proper ending for *Superman*. We were working with the writers and with Tom Mankiewicz who was working with Donner, and we didn't have an ending. And we were talking also at that time with Richard Lester, who had come on board as an additional producer. We were thinking, 'What can we do for an ending?' And then I remembered those conferences with Mario Puzo and Carmine Infantino. In one of those conferences, Puzo said, 'Oh, I've got an idea to create tension – let's kill Lois.' And Carmine went crazy: 'Come on, you can't do that!' Puzo said, 'No, but of course we'll resuscitate her somehow.' And so we came up with this idea: we'll kill Lois and then use an ending that was originally written as the ending of *Superman II*, in which Superman reverses time. Originally at the end of *Superman II*, a lot of damage has been done by the three Kryptonian villains on Earth, and so to repair it all Superman just reverses time and the world is repaired. So we used that reversing of time and the death of Lois as the ending of *Superman: The Movie*. Well, that idea came out of a conference we had with Lester. That was the kind of intervention he had on the movie.

GB: *The decision to replace Donner with Lester remains controversial. But it has been reported that you did offer Donner the chance to finish shooting* Superman II.
PS: I did. Yeah, yeah. And I know Donner attempted to make quote unquote 'his' version [*Superman II: The Richard Donner Cut*], which used in the region of 50 per cent of recovered footage that he had shot for *Superman II*. But (a) there was footage that was no good, and (b) there was footage that wasn't even supposed to be footage – it was just taken from screen tests. You know, God bless him. I know there is always this discussion of 'Why didn't he direct *Superman II*?' But a lot of water has gone under the bridge. The result of *Superman: The Movie*, despite all the difficulties and all the headaches and all the overages, is that he made a good movie. There's no question.

> "Chris Reeve came in to audition, and he did the two parts fabulously. But both Richard Donner and I said, 'He's fantastic but he's so skinny. He's like a string bean. How will anyone believe that he is Superman?'"

ILYA SALKIND

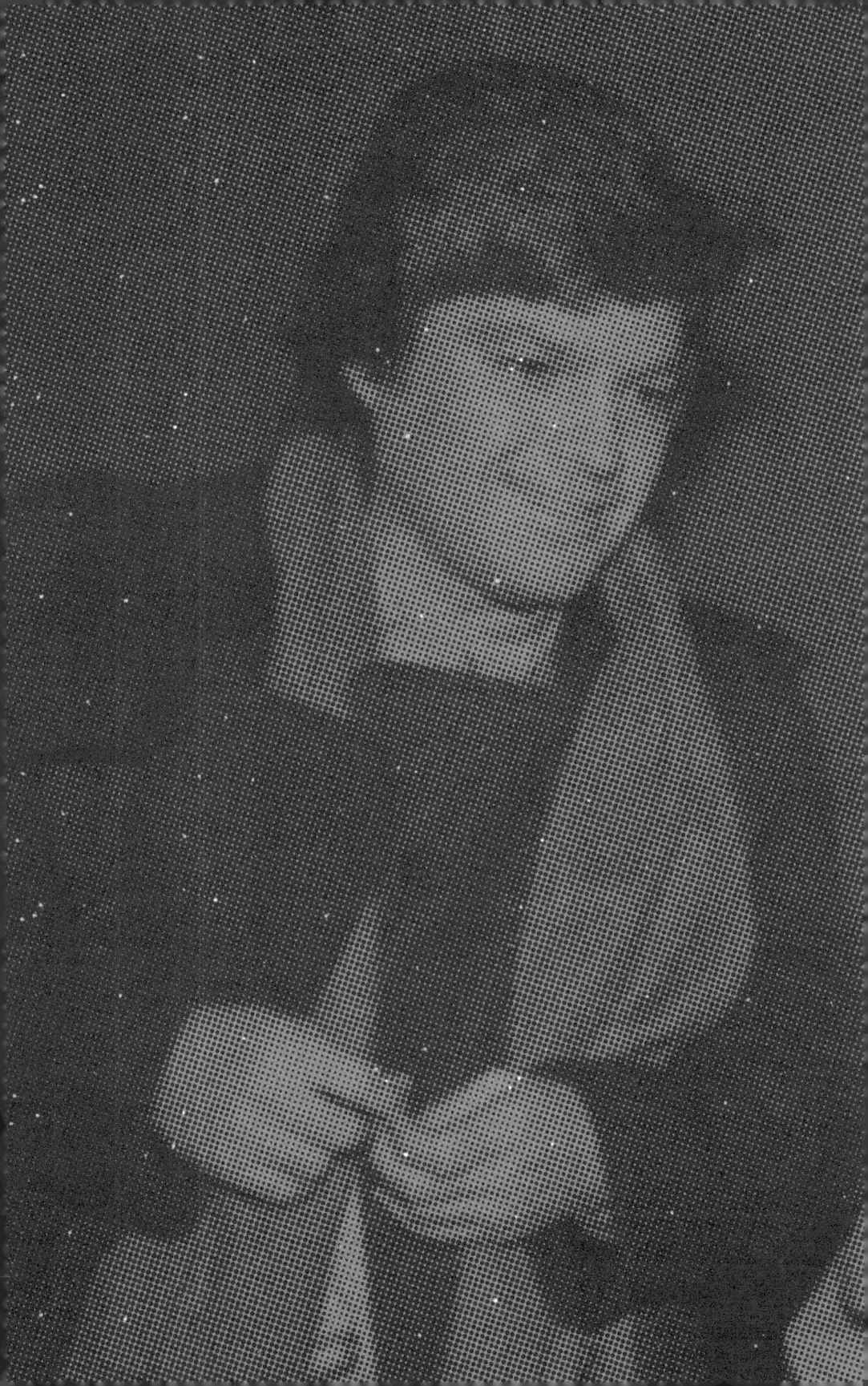

ILYA SALKIND
EXECUTIVE PRODUCER

Gary Bettinson: You produced Superman *along with Pierre Spengler and your father, Alexander Salkind. How was the division of labour organized among the three of you?*
Ilya Salkind: My father raised all the money. I was 95 per cent involved in the casting of actors and I was the one with the closest relationship with the director. Pierre, who is my best friend, was much more involved in the line producing aspect, overseeing all the technicians. But obviously, as we are extremely close friends, many times we would collaborate on different tasks. It wasn't like I was in one corner and he was in another corner.

GB: Can you tell me about the casting process? I gather that DC Comics approved Dustin Hoffman for the role of Superman.
IS: Yes, absolutely. He was considered. We met him at the Cannes Film Festival. He was not considered for the role of Superman; he was considered for Lex Luthor. We never thought of him for Superman. Dustin is a fabulous actor but casting him as Superman wouldn't have worked. You needed a guy that looked more like the comic-book character. So we considered James Caan, Jon Voight, Warren Beatty and finally – I think he was one of the last we considered – I offered the part to Robert Redford, who was very hot and one of the top stars in the world. Thank God he turned it down because if he had accepted, frankly, I don't think the movie would have had the same kind of impact that it had with Christopher Reeve. After Dustin turned down the part of Luthor, I came up with a new idea. I said to my father, 'Look, let's forget about trying to find a star to play Superman; we're never going to find an actor that looks like him and can play him well. Let's cast Jor-El and Lex Luthor with stars big enough to carry the film so that we can get an unknown actor to play the main part.' My father agreed, and the first guy I offered it to was Paul Newman. Warren Cowan, who was one of the top press agents at the time, represented Newman. He said to me, 'Look, why don't you offer Paul a part in the film?' And I said 'Alright', because Redford had turned us down, and I was already in a state of complete panic. So I offered it to Newman. I said, 'We will offer you $2.5 million to

play Superman.' It was a gigantic amount at that time. Newman was still young then, in his late-40s, and he still looked great. I offered him $2.5 million to play Superman or to play Jor-El or to play Lex Luthor. Well, okay. He turned it down. So then I was literally suicidal.

GB: What did you do?
IS: After Newman said no, I was completely desperate. And then a very crazy thing happened. An old agent named Kurt Frings, who was possibly one of the greatest agents in the business at that time, called me on the phone. He represented Audrey Hepburn, he represented Rex Harrison and he was connected somehow with Brando. So Kurt calls me at the Beverly Hills Hotel and says, 'Ilya, Ilya, I can get you Marlon Brando.' I said, 'What, are you crazy, Kurt?' And he called three, four, five times. He was an agent, after all – agents don't give up. And finally at the fifth time, I said 'Okay, alright, so you'll get me Brando – how are you going to get him?' He said, 'My girlfriend, Marie, had an affair with him, and I guarantee you she will get him to read the script. But he will want $2.7 million.' I said, 'My God! Are you completely crazy?' We're talking 1977, right? I'd offered, as I said, $2.5 million to Newman, but this was even more money. However, I called my father in Paris and said, 'We can get Brando but he wants $2.7 million – what do we do?' It took my father just three seconds to consider it, and then he said 'Go for it.' So I called Kurt and sent him the script. The next morning he calls back. 'Marie got Brando to read the script in the toilet, and he will do it – he will play Superman's father.' I said, 'My God, that's fantastic.' 'Yes, he will do it but he wants 11.3 per cent of the gross on top of the $2.7 million.' I said, 'Oh, come on Kurt, you're crazy – that's unheard of; it's impossible.' So I call my father and, again, about a quarter of a second later he said, 'Okay, go for it.' And that was it. The moment we got Brando the production was like a train going along. Getting Brando, and then Hackman, gave me the opportunity to look for an unknown actor to play Superman.

GB: How did you find Christopher Reeve?
IS: Our casting director, Lynn Stalmaster, suddenly said, 'Okay, there's a young kid, very young, he's 6'4", he looks great, and you should meet him.' And Chris Reeve came in and he did the two parts fabulously. But both Donner and I said, 'Yeah, he's fantastic but he's so skinny. He's like a string bean. How will anyone believe that he is Superman?' In those days the Motion Picture Almanac published little pictures of actors, and I was looking at that almanac every day. I would look and pass Chris Reeve's face every time. I thought, 'My God, he looks great, he's got this big neck, and Superman has to have this kind of look.' So I convinced Donner, who was very reluctant, to screen-test Reeve. Chris came to London and of course he was fantastic, and that was it. I convinced Donner, I said, 'He can bulk up.' And Chris started working out crazily, with very, very strong willpower. He started working out with Dave Prowse who had played Darth Vader in *Star*

Wars, and I think he built 30 pounds of muscle. As I said, he was 6'4" so he became this gigantic guy.

GB: You say that you met with Reeve in London. When did the base of production shift from Italy to England?
IS: As I said, the production started rolling once we hired Brando. Then we were in Rome for about a year-and-a-half preparing with Guy Hamilton. But we had a lot of problems in Rome. I love Italy and I love to eat there, but I would say that to work with the Italians is a different story. [Laughs.] They do have a little tendency to exaggerate. And so finally we realized that nothing was going to happen there, and we decided to move to England because in England the pound was very, very low – boy, I think a pound was a dollar – so it was very cheap. And *all* the best technicians were available. I mean, the great guys who had done Kubrick's *2001*, the guys who had done James Bond, all of them. And actually we ended up having a fantastic, unbelievable crew for *Superman* – John Barry, the set designer of *Star Wars*; Geoffrey Unsworth, who had done *2001*, was the lighting cameraman; Derek Meddings, who had done the Bond films, was in charge of model effects. It was just incredible. And they were all available because there was a lack of movies in England at the time. Production output was very low. And the pound was very low as well. So we moved to London. We had gotten Brando and Hackman before that. We already had them when Donner came on-board. Donner, by the way, had taken the reins because poor Guy Hamilton could not go to England because of tax reasons. In England, they would charge people who made money 99 per cent of taxes – unbelievable. So you had guys like The Rolling Stones leaving the country and going to live in other places. It was madness. And of course Guy Hamilton just couldn't do it. Now, why did we choose Dick Donner? That's another story. My father and I were wondering who we were going to choose to direct. We had these two gigantic stars in Brando and Hackman, we had a script by the Newmans and Benton that was getting very close to what we wanted, and then we said, 'Okay, let's see what's around.'

GB: Wasn't Steven Spielberg on your radar at this time?
IS: Oh, absolutely. We were based in Paris then, and every week one of the big agencies was calling me, saying, 'Look, there's this young kid, he's very good. He's doing *Jaws*.' Steven wanted to direct *Superman*; he was a fanatic of sci-fi. So I went immediately to see *Duel* and *Sugarland Express*, and I thought they were very good. I went to my father and I said, 'This young kid Spielberg, he's doing *Jaws*, it's going to be a gigantic hit. We should take him.' And my father said, 'Let's wait until the big fish picture opens.' Well, *Jaws* came out and it was an enormous hit. Then my father started saying, 'Oh my God, let's get Spielberg, let's get Spielberg!' So I called Spielberg's agent and this time he took about three weeks to answer. He finally answered and I said, 'Look, we'd like Spielberg to direct the film,' and he said 'Oh, let me talk to him.' He promptly changed his tone –

before, it was 'Take this kid, take this kid,' but now he said, 'Let me talk to him.' Then he came back and said, 'Yeah, well, Steven might do it but he wants to make a crazy Hellzapoppin musical out of it' – which was a wonderful way of saying, 'Go fly a kite.' So, no – it didn't happen. Later Steven ended up working with Donner on many films.[9]

GB: What qualities did you perceive in Donner that were appropriate for Superman?
IS: Well, I think a combination of things. For me, the way I judge a director is if he has the ability to shift between really different styles in the same film. If you look at *Superman*, it's a very good example of that because you have the Krypton scenes, which are bold sci-fi; then you have this Andrew Wyeth kind of beautiful Kent Farm in Smallville; and then you get into that very quick tempo, when Superman meets Lois Lane and Perry White in Metropolis. That ability to switch styles is what I try to find with a director. And in *The Omen* I saw that. It really is a film that keeps you calm at the beginning and just builds up, and at the end you're completely paralyzed by terror. So that was one thing. But I think there was a totality of reasons for selecting Donner. He was able to handle a veteran star like Gregory Peck; he was able to handle the suspense; he handled the characters, even the kid [Damien Thorn, played by Harvey Stephens], very well. I mean, the whole thing worked. Every level of *The Omen* worked.

GB: How did Donner's approach to the Superman material differ from that of Guy Hamilton?
IS: Well, I give Donner a lot of credit; he brought in Tom Mankiewicz and we all worked on the script. But even so, a lot of stuff that is in the final film was written by Guy and the Newmans and Benton and myself. There have been all these stories from Donner and Mankiewicz that we wanted to make the movie camp and funny. And yes, there was one scene where Superman is walking in the street and he sees Telly Savalas as Kojak, who says 'Heya baby.'[10] It was absurd. Now, I don't know who wrote that – I don't know if it was the Newmans or Benton – but it was in there. And that's a line that Donner and Mankiewicz later would point to and say, 'Yes, the original script was a parody, it was a comedy.' No – that scene would have never stayed in the film. I was going to take it out. See, what a lot of people don't realize is that a film is an evolution. You don't start with a perfect finished script. It doesn't happen. The thing with Superman is that you must laugh with the characters, not at them. If you laugh at them, you're finished – then the whole thing just becomes a joke.

GB: Why did you decide to move the Superman production from Shepperton Studios to Pinewood Studios? Was Shepperton too small for a production of this scale?
IS: Yes. At one point there were eleven full units shooting simultaneously. There were so many units working on *Superman* that we had to add Twickenham Studios as well. At one point we were working at three studios at the same time. Unbelievable. We did a

small part of the film at Twickenham; we did a lot at Shepperton; and then we became completely Pinewood people, because we did all the films after *Superman* at Pinewood: *Superman II* and *III*, *Santa Claus: The Movie* and *Supergirl* were all filmed there.

GB: You were very much an active presence during shooting. Did you form strong relationships with the cast and crew?
IS: I had a very, very strong connection with Christopher Reeve. With Gene Hackman – we spoke three or four times, we shook hands, but there was no connection. That's the difference. Some actors you connect with in more than a business way. If you don't develop a rapport with an actor, it doesn't mean that you hate each other. It just means there is no real connection. With Christopher, he and I were very close. I was more than affected when he had the accident [in 1995]. I mean, it was absolutely traumatic for me. Very painful. What happened to him is just unthinkable.

GB: How did Richard Lester become involved in Superman: The Movie*?*
IS: Donner just couldn't make up his mind. I give him credit, because *Superman* was a very, very difficult movie to make. Donner was great. The only thing was that sometimes he just couldn't make up his mind, and we went over-budget and over-budget and over-budget. Then it got to a point where we had a very difficult rapport, and that's when he started literally insulting us. After the success of *Superman: The Movie*, he was really not pleasant. In Army Archerd's column in *Variety*, Donner started saying not pleasant things about us – such as, you know, 'They're idiots' or 'I'll do the sequel my way.' Donner and I had a lot of problems, but I fired him because he was saying horrible things about my father and myself. I said to my father, 'We can't work with this guy; it's going to be impossible.' That's why we took Lester, who had worked with us on *Musketeers*. Now, Lester was very instrumental in many things on *Superman: The Movie*. Actually, he was *the* most instrumental in saying, 'Drop the second film.' That was Lester – it was not Donner, Pierre, me, my father or Warners. Lester said, 'If you don't postpone the second film, you'll never finish the first one in time,' because we had already missed the original summer deadline. So we already had this catastrophe of missing the release date; plus the film was going over-budget in a horrible way. Lester was fantastic as a go-between, and he came up with this great idea so that we were able to open the first Superman movie by Christmas of 1978.

GB: You launched the promotional campaign for Superman: The Movie *years before the film's theatrical release. The pre-release advertising campaigns at the Cannes Film Festival, for instance, have become rather legendary.*
IS: Yes. Years later, there was an article in *Variety* that said, 'What has become of the days when the Salkinds were in Cannes and doing all these incredible things?' It's true – we gained an enormous amount of publicity at the Cannes Film Festival in 1974, where

we had planes flying overhead [trailing a Superman banner]. One year, we announced Mario Puzo and Guy Hamilton – who had done *Goldfinger*, and who was the first director we hired for *Superman* – and we had fifteen or sixteen planes flying over Cannes, and a yacht with 'Superman' written on it. It was very, very impressive. We made sure that everybody knew about the film.

GB: Similarly, the marketing and merchandising of **Superman** *were on an unprecedented scale.*
IS: Well, I'll give credit to Warners. They got very excited when they saw the first rushes. And they even delegated a special guy called Bob Rosenthal, who was representing all the different sides of Warners – the merchandising, the comic books, everything. He was a liaison for all that. So Warners was very instrumental in making the movie really a gigantic event. For example, they are the ones who organized for *Time* and *Newsweek* to preview the film. We had already cut the first film together, so the critics saw the first film, and we got the cover of *Newsweek* and the banner of *Time*. That was a fantastic moment. In those days, it was unbelievable to get the cover of *Time*.

GB: Is it true that after terminating Donner's contract, you brought back Guy Hamilton to work on **Superman II** *before finally hiring Lester to direct?*
IS: Yes, we tried again to get Guy to direct, but again it didn't work out. Guy was wonderful.

GB: What qualities did Lester bring to **Superman II** *that marked him off from Donner?*
IS: Usually, Donner would literally do what I would say, or what I was able to convince him to do. Lester was a little different, because I would come up with a problem and he would come up with an idea to solve the problem.

GB: Can you recall an example from **Superman II**?
IS: Yes. There is a scene in *Superman II* where Superman goes to an island to pick some flowers for Lois Lane. In post-production, we were in the music sessions with Ken Thorne, a wonderful musician who took John Williams' score and re-orchestrated it. At one point, Lester took a piece of music that in my opinion didn't work at all for that sequence. We had a confrontation about it, which I won, and he adapted. He would come with solutions. In that case, the solution was putting the piece of music that I wanted over the scene, whereas before he had used something completely different. Also, Lester adapted himself very much to everything that Dick had already shot for *Superman II*, so it went very well.

GB: How do you regard the Superman sequels today?
IS: Of course, *Superman: The Movie* is fantastic. But, of all the Superman films, I will tell you frankly: I prefer *Superman II*.

GB: Whose cut do you consider superior?
IS: By far the Lester cut. By far. I literally had nothing to do with Donner's cut. We still had control with Warners [in 2006], and I agreed that Donner could do his own cut of *Superman II*. Why didn't I like the Donner cut? Because they did something which I think is absolutely crazy: Superman makes love to Lois *before* losing his powers. That doesn't make any sense. The whole point of the second film is that he loses his powers because he wants to live as a mortal with Lois.[11] Well, if you look at the Donner cut, Superman makes love with her *before* and then he loses his powers *after*. What's the point? I don't know why Donner did that. For me, it was just so wrong. Look, I give him credit – he got his cut, you know? And I'm sure he felt good about it. But the whole structure of the film goes down, because the *only* reason that Superman chooses to lose his powers is for love. Why would he choose to lose his powers *after* making love to Lois? It just doesn't make any sense.

GB: And **Superman III***?*
IS: *Superman III* was a much bigger hit than people think. It still made $40 million in rentals, so that means about $120 million in the theatres. It was a pretty big hit. But I was perhaps getting a little bit less involved, a little bit more relaxed about the whole thing. And perhaps I became a little bit softer with Lester, in making him do a little bit too much slapstick. I was way more hands-on with Dick Donner. You know, it was a question of tonality. In *Superman II*, Lester was right on. In *Superman III*, he went a little too far, and I was guilty of being a little bit asleep, perhaps. In the opening scene of *Superman III*, which is a great Hellzapoppin thing, it's not the same style as the previous Superman films.[12] On the other hand, the true fans adore the scene in the junkyard between Clark Kent and Superman. That scene is one of the high points of the entire series of Superman films produced by my father and me. After *Superman III*, we got to a point where we said, 'Alright, let's do *Supergirl*.' Meanwhile, of course, Cannon was destroying the whole franchise with *Superman IV*.

GB: You sold the Superman film rights in 1985?
IS: Yes, to this weird, crazy group called Cannon Films. We sold the rights for, at that time, five million bucks. So now Cannon had the rights to do *Superman IV*. And if you look at the film you'll see in the credits: 'The film was created by Alexander Salkind' – which is horrible, but I can't take it out. [Laughs.] As you well know, *Superman IV* was certainly not a success. I'm trying to be nice here, but…it is certainly not a film that reviewers consider a great film. I mean, frankly, the film is an abomination.

GB: Where did your father rank Superman *in the context of his overall career? Did he consider it an artistic highlight?*
IS: Well, he did, because it was such a gigantic hit. And critically too – the reviews were fantastic. He was not only happy but very excited that it was such a gigantic hit.

GB: And where do you rank Superman *in your own body of work?*
IS: A lot of people ask me, 'What is your favourite film that you've produced?' and everybody thinks it's going to be *Superman*, but I say, 'No, it's *The Four Musketeers*.' For me, *The Four Musketeers* is really my favourite of the films I've made. But you know, that's my own opinion. A lot of people say, 'Oh, come on – *Superman* is the best.' And yes, of course, *Superman* is fantastic. I was completely passionate about the film, as I was passionate for *The Three Musketeers* and *The Four Musketeers*. Before *Superman*, there were no comic-book films. There had been a very lousy little *Batman* where they literally adapted the TV series and put it on the big screen.[13] They didn't create a mythos for the character like we did for *Superman*, which became influential on every film that you see now. Nowadays you see, what? Three or four comic-book films a year? *Iron Man*, *Avengers*...it doesn't stop. And the horror of *Batman v. Superman* – my God, how could they do a film like that? I still don't understand. Really, our intention when we made *Superman* was to put it in its own category. And I've said it before, I'll say it again: so far, the best Superman at this point in time is Christopher Reeve, and that's it. You know, Henry Cavill is OK, Brandon Routh is very nice, but come on – Reeve is in a league of his own.

"The audience had to believe it. That was the slogan on Superman's advertising programs: 'You'll believe a man can fly.' And that was my mission: you had to believe a man can fly or else there was no movie."

RICHARD DONNER

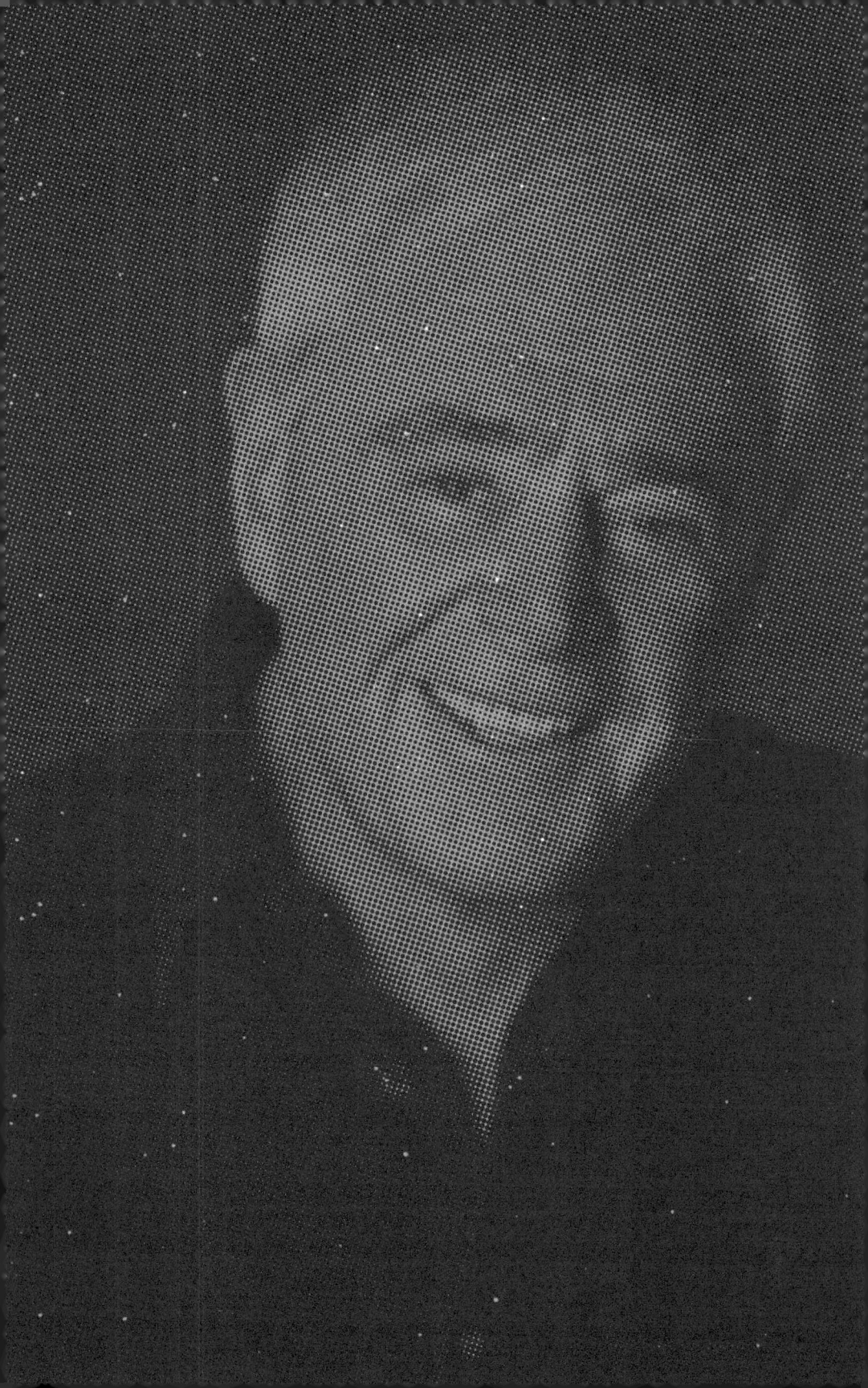

RICHARD DONNER
DIRECTOR

Gary Bettinson: The Salkinds offered you one million dollars to direct a Superman script written by Mario Puzo, with Marlon Brando and Gene Hackman attached to star. That sounds like an irresistible offer, but did you have any reservations about accepting the assignment?

Richard Donner: I had major reservations about it until I read what they had written. And – it sounds stupid – but I decided I would do the movie to defend Superman from the foreigners. They were doing a movie about Superman, but to me it was wrong. They hadn't captured what that character was all about, and what for years of history the character had represented for kids and adults alike. And so you might say I did the movie in defence of Superman.

GB: Did you collaborate with Puzo at all, or had he already left the project when you came on board?

RD: He had left. I came on board only on the basis that I could bring a writer on to rewrite the script. And that was Tom Mankiewicz. Now, the Writers Guild, in their inimitable tastelessness and defence of nothingness, wouldn't give Tom the screen credit he deserved. His credit should have been: 'Written by Tom Mankiewicz.' But the Writers Guild wouldn't allow it. So we gave him a ghost credit called 'Creative Consultant,' but anybody that knew the problems and the fixings and the makings of *Superman* knew that it was Tom Mankiewicz who wrote it.

GB: What qualities did you believe Mankiewicz would bring to the screenplay? Why hire him above other writers?

RD: Well, he brought verisimilitude. He brought the sense of reality that I wanted for it. He brought a humour that came out of the characters' situation, rather than the forced comedy of the earlier draft. The original script had no reality. That's why I emphasized the word 'verisimilitude' – the story had to have a sense of its own reality. Tom brought that reality to the script. And he brought the unrequited love relationship, the

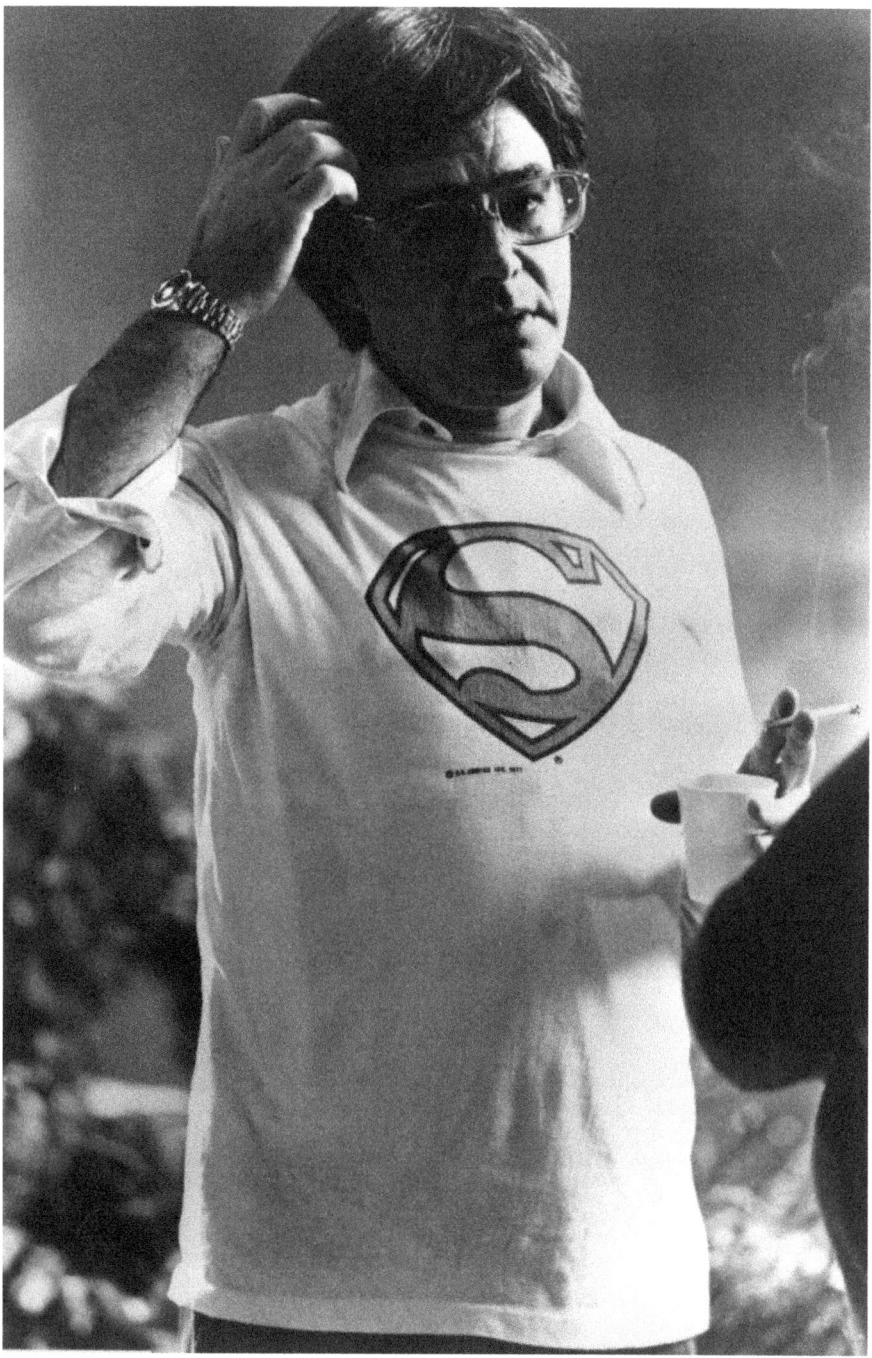

Figure 2: Richard Donner on the set of *Superman*. Photo: Moviestore/REX/Shutterstock.

general drama of Clark and Superman being in love with the same woman. He brought everything. He was there to write, and so I kept him in England during the shooting of *Superman*. He would come to the set every day, because he was planning to be a director himself one day. And he eventually did direct movies, and he did a good job.[14] On *Superman*, he was like my other set of eyes. If I missed something, he spotted it. Tom made a very difficult process easier. He was really a dear buddy, a great friend, and I'd known him for a hundred years. He has since passed on.[15]

GB: As part of your preparation, did the two of you read the Superman comic books or revisit the 1950s television series?
RD: Well, not very much. I mean, that was the kind of preparation that had been done before we came onto the film. Tom and I kind of wanted to get as far away from that comic-book background as possible. Like I say, we were going for reality.

GB: You had already worked with a veteran film star (Gregory Peck) on **The Omen.** *Did this experience prepare you for working with Marlon Brando? Did it give you the confidence to handle a star of his magnitude?*
RD: No, I never had the confidence. I still don't. I mean, movie stars are human beings – they have their foibles, their realities, their good side, their bad side. Each one gives you a new insight once you go to work with them, and so you never know what to expect. Those two guys, Peck and Brando, were an extraordinary pleasure to work with. Great education, great delight. They had such self-confidence. I had no more problem with them than I would have had with anybody else.

GB: How did Brando respond to **Superman: The Movie** *when it was finished? Did you watch the film with him or screen it for him?*
RD: No, I didn't. But he called me afterwards and sent me a lovely little gift and a thank-you, and he said he was thoroughly entertained – which is priceless to me.

GB: Margot Kidder told me that she and Christopher Reeve had very different methods of working. How did you handle their contrasting approaches?
RD: You know, they just loved each other. Margot treated him like her kid brother. She mothered him through that movie. And I let them do their thing. They both seemed to respect the direction I would give them. But it was a very mutual relationship between all of us. Very happy. Breezy.

GB: Later in his life, Christopher Reeve recalled telling you of his plans to direct a film (**In the Gloaming**). *According to Reeve, you replied 'So what's new?' (Reeve 1999: 258). Was Reeve creatively immersed in the making of* **Superman** *beyond the consideration of his own performance?*

RD: Oh sure. He was with me every minute that he wasn't shooting. He was always asking questions; he was always interested. I made sure that he was not hesitant to make suggestions. And if he got something out of that, fine. Maybe he learned what you shouldn't do as well as what you should. [Laughs.]

GB: I'm curious to know how you came to cast Terence Stamp, who was virtually living in exile in the 1970s. It was inspired casting.
RD: Oh God, I have to be honest: I don't remember. There is a great chance it was [UK casting director] Mary Selway's idea, because she was one of the great casting agents. She was a very special woman.

GB: The special effects units had initiated a series of flying tests under Guy Hamilton's aegis, all of which you rejected. In what ways did these experiments fall short of your requirements?
RD: The simple answer is that they weren't believable. The audience had to believe it. That was the slogan on the advertising programs: 'You'll believe a man can fly.' And that was my mission: you had to believe a man can fly or else there was no movie. That's what we put our concerted effort into. It took a year before we accepted our first flying shot. A year – that's a *long* time when you're making a movie.

GB: Did your faith ever waver?
RD: No, because we would not stop until we had it. And I surrounded myself with the best talent. In England at that point, they had the most talented effects people and creative people in the motion picture industry. I went out of my way to find what I considered to be the very, very best that was available. And it turned out that I hit it on the nose. They were all just geniuses, and they made it happen for me. You know, we had five or six units at all times: there were units for the flying, for the models, for the painted backgrounds – everything. So many units. Every day at dailies we would see each unit's efforts, and we could see the flying effects improving. The flying effort gradually became the most important task, because we were running out of time to complete the movie. [Visual effects artist] Denys Coop came on the movie for a month as a favour to Geoffrey Unsworth. I had explained to Geoffrey what I needed the flying effects to be, and I asked him, 'How are we going to do it?' Geoffrey said, 'Let me see if I can get Denys to come on board, just to help us get started.' Well, it ended up that Denys stayed with us for two years! So it was all a concerted effort by a lot of amazing, amazing people. One of the great honours of my life was working with all those people. I mean, you look at those names on the credits – they're almost all gone now – and you just come away thinking, 'Wow.'

GB: You reportedly had an affectionate but feisty collaboration with editor Stuart Baird. What were your main areas of disagreement?
RD: It's what I loved about him. Stuart couldn't be cajoled into doing anything that he felt wasn't right. And I myself often wanted something different than Stuart wanted, and we would fight over it. For him to win, he had to prove something – cut some footage together and show me. And 99 per cent of the time, he was right. We wouldn't shoot on Saturdays, and so I usually spent Saturdays going to Pinewood and sitting with Stuart, going through our footage and arguing and fighting with him. But I think there was a great mutual respect between both of us.

GB: So you were editing the film as you were shooting?
RD: Oh yeah. We had to, because we had terrible [delivery] dates. We had to make sure that we were always progressing as we were shooting, because we knew that one of those days the producers were going to turn around and give us an honest date for when we had to deliver the movie to the studio. And so we worked constantly.

GB: In his autobiography, Christopher Reeve recalls you counselling him about directing movies. You told him, he writes, that 'the first time you see the film put together, you come away depressed and wonder if there is any hope of fixing it' (Reeve 1999: 253). Did you have this reaction the first time you saw Superman *cut together?*
RD: The answer is: I've had that reaction on every movie I made. You always look at it and think, 'Oh my God, what did I do? I'll never work again! This is terrible.' But then you go to work on it, and if you're lucky you have somebody as stabilizing as Stuart to make sure you keep your head on your shoulders. And you go to work.

GB: Do you have that sense of deflation even when you edit the film while you're shooting?
RD: As you're making it? No, because you can always go back into the edit room when you're shooting and make things different. So I never really had a feeling of 'I'm in trouble,' because I could always go in and clean something up the next morning on the scene we were still shooting. So no, that doesn't happen that much when you're still in the process of filming. It's in post-production when that sense of depression sets in.

GB: Superman *was an immense undertaking. With so many technical challenges to overcome, and with pressure from the producers, how did you combat self-doubt?*
RD: Well, the thing is, you didn't have the time to doubt yourself. You had to just keep going. You had to not so much convince but encourage people – and yourself – that you were doing the right thing. You really didn't know when you were saying those things whether you were being honest or desperate, but you knew you had to keep going and believe that what you were doing was right. You had to believe it. You talked yourself into it. There was no time to doubt yourself or others.

GB: Was that a very lonely process, or did you have someone to turn to for counsel? Did Tom Mankiewicz fill that role for you?
RD: Oh yeah. Tom lived in a hotel in Mayfair, and I had an apartment in Chelsea. We would drive home with the driver from the studio every night at the end of work, and that is all we'd ever talk about: 'What was today like? How did we do? Did we go in the right direction? Did we make any mistakes? Of course we did. How do we get out of them? What do we do?' If there was something from the day's work that stood out as bad, we'd discuss how to rectify it. Or if we had done a good day's work, we'd go through the whole thing and talk about why it worked. Sometimes we would go into work the next day and make some major changes based on our discussions from the night before. We kind of created the movie driving in and out of work. The ride home in that car was always an extreme education.

GB: What conversations did you have with John Williams before he composed the Superman score? Did you give him any specific guidelines?
RD: There are no guidelines; there are emotions. John is a genius when it comes to film interpretation. We did what is called 'spotting' – we would look at the film together when we were doing our temp version of the music track, and we'd work out which moments we felt deserved music. He listened, he gave some thoughts about it, and then he went away. I felt satisfied that we were both thinking the same way. Later on, he came back with his score, and he stunned me into oblivion. We were in the studio where we were recording, and John was on the stage with the London Symphony Orchestra. The orchestra started to play the main Superman theme, and it was just God-given. Unreal. I thought, 'Oh my God, this is beautiful music. This is great.' John is and was quite the person. He is one of the greats of our time.

GB: **Superman: The Movie** *is dedicated to Geoffrey Unsworth. I understand that his method of working was quite meticulous. Would you say that he set a standard of quality for others working on the film?*
RD: Oh, by far. He was the master. What he did was a reflection on the entire movie. He was loved and respected by everybody that was on that set – and obviously, by many, many more people that weren't. He was a very special man and a dear, dear friend. Same thing with [production designer] John Barry. John was a genius. John would come to you with ideas and you'd think, 'Oh, where did that come from? How could he have seen something that I didn't?' John was a unique human being. One feels blessed that the producers gave me the opportunity to learn from him, and to just be in his presence. As I said, there wasn't a person on the *Superman* crew – and there wasn't an actor in that movie – that I would replace with somebody else if I had the opportunity. They were all perfect.

GB: *Do you recall how Jerry Siegel and Joe Shuster reacted after watching* **Superman: The Movie?**

RD: I'll tell you how they reacted. During the years that they wrote the Superman comic-book series, they had these magnificent statues of Superman commissioned. These statues were about two-feet high. And the night of the movie opening, Siegel and Shuster brought their statue and gave it to me. I cherish it and still have it to this day, obviously. Interestingly enough, last year the studio gave [comic-book writer] Geoff Johns – who used to be my assistant and has become one of my closest friends – the only other statue that we know of. So it will stay in the heritage of our friendship forever.

GB: *An extended television cut of* **Superman:** *The Movie was recently released on Blu-ray, and there are now several versions of the film in circulation. Which version do you consider to be the definitive director's cut?*

RD: The original cut that was released in theatres was my cut, and anything else I had nothing to do with. That long television version had nothing to do with what I thought was the proper version. If there are other versions floating around, I have no idea where they came from. At certain points in your life, you lose control of a film. I thought it was foolish – everything that I had taken out of the film, they put back in. It was stupid. But anything for money.

GB: *Its title notwithstanding, was the Donner cut of* **Superman II** *truly your cut of the film?*

RD: Basically, no. What happened was there was a fan movement afoot that wanted to see what my cut would have been if the Salkinds, in their inimitable good taste, had allowed me to finish my movie. What was released was *The Richard Donner Cut*, but it's really not mine because there was no way of finishing the cut and getting all the pieces together that were not in the original. So it was just kind of this thing put together with spit and polish. It wasn't my version because we didn't complete my photography, but it was a pleasure to at least get out there what the intentions of the film would have been. The fellow who directed it, Michael Thau, saw it through different eyes. That movie is the way he presented it, and I was thrilled that I could in some way show you what I thought the movie should have been.

GB: *Are you now reconciled with Ilya Salkind and Pierre Spengler?*

RD: Oh sure. Time heals everything. Things like that are not worth holding onto with a bad spirit or a bad thought.

GB: *Water under the bridge?*

RD: Right, exactly.

GB: *It has been claimed that the producers invited you to direct* **Superman II.** *There seems to be some confusion about this.*
RD: No, it's not true. I was sent a telegram that just said, 'Your services are no longer needed.'

GB: *Was Brando disappointed to be cut from the sequel?*
RD: I don't think he gave a damn.

GB: *He had no emotional attachment to the film?*
RD: I don't know. I never got to talk to him to that degree afterwards. If he did, I think he kept it to himself, pretty much – although his confidants might be able to tell you something different. He was a very interesting man.

GB: *Is it true that after the Salkinds left the Superman franchise, Christopher Reeve asked you to direct* **Superman IV?** *If so, why did you reject his invitation?*
RD: I have no recollection of that. [Laughs.]

GB: *It must be gratifying that audiences continue to appreciate* **Superman: The Movie.**
RD: Yeah, I'm very proud of the movie. I get very high on audiences' reactions to the film.

GB: *Do you plan to direct again? There have recently been rumours of a* **Lethal Weapon** *sequel.*[16]
RD: I was thinking about it, but Warner Brothers decided they don't want to make it. It's too bad. I think we could have done a wonderful film. But Warner Brothers have decided…well, let me put it this way, their legal division, their monetary group, have decided they don't want to invest in it. That's showbiz!

GB: *Would you want to direct another project in the future?*
RD: No, I don't think so. The only thing I would have done was *Lethal Weapon*, because I had a wonderful story and I think the audiences would have loved it. I think I would have liked to have put it to bed for a finale. But that…is…*it*. I'm having too much of a wonderful life, and my world as it is today is terrific. It would take a lot to make me give it up, and I can't think of anything that I would do besides that.

"Christopher Reeve and I had fights. If I'd improvised something, Chris would cut take and say, 'You can't do that.' And I'd yell, 'Shut up! Don't tell me how to act. This is your first movie and my tenth!'"

MARGOT KIDDER

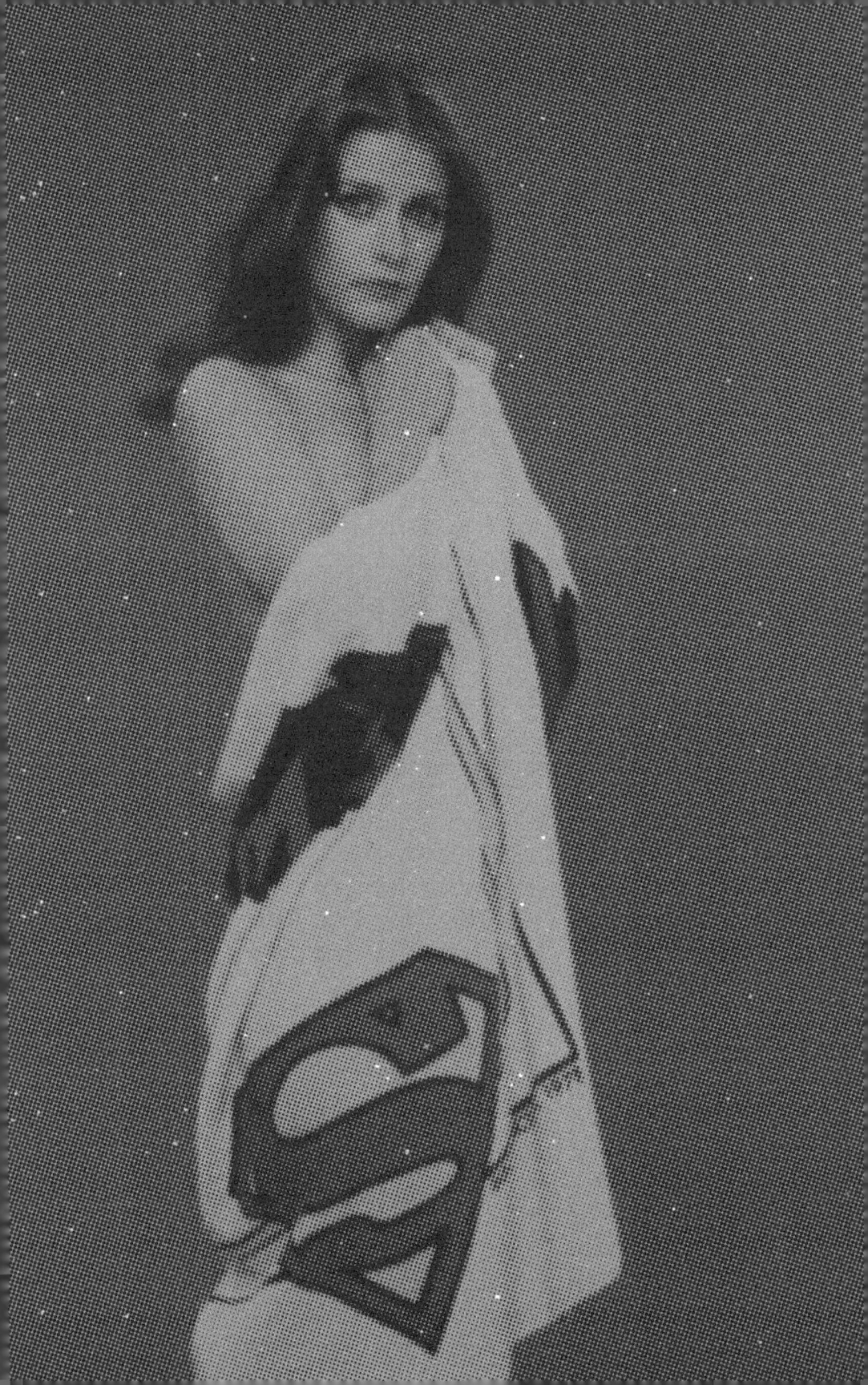

MARGOT KIDDER
LOIS LANE

Gary Bettinson: Can you clarify how you came to audition for **Superman**? *Some reports state that your agent, Rick Nicita, put you forward for the audition, while according to* Rolling Stone *(Klinger 1981: 21), it was Christopher Reeve who suggested you for the role of Lois Lane.*
Margot Kidder: Christopher didn't suggest me at all. That part's not true, no.

GB: Do you know the factors that led to your screen test?
MK: Well, honestly, I was here in Montana in a very bad marriage, and I knew that I didn't have the strength to get out of it on my own. I knew that I had to go to work in order to get my self-esteem back. And so I actually called Rick, who I hadn't met yet, and said, 'I need you to be my agent and I need to work right away.' And he said, 'Shouldn't we have a meeting?' I said, 'Get me an audition. I'll come down there, do the audition, and meet you.' I hadn't heard about *Superman*. I'd never read the comics. I was brought up in Northern Canada in very remote mining camps, and I wasn't allowed to read comic books. So I didn't know much about it. Anyway, I flew to Los Angeles and met with Tom Mankiewicz and Dick Donner, and they loved what I did with the scenes. I met with Rick, and he said, 'Great, I'll sign you on.' A week later, when I got back to Montana, Donner and Mank [Mankiewicz] called from London and said, 'Would you come and screen test?' I said, 'You bet.' And I got the part.

GB: Do you recall the actual experience of doing the screen test?
MK: Oh yeah. I remember I was quite nervous. I do remember thinking all the way over there on the plane: 'Okay, you *have* to get this part because your marriage is so bad, you've got to get out of it. So what do you think you have to do to get the part?' The first thing I realized was I had to make it seem as if I really, really loved Superman. And I knew that was the key – acting as if I were madly in love with Superman. By then, I had read the script – I still hadn't read any comics, except one – and I knew that I had to have this thing that a lot of women have, which is when you're around a guy who loves you

too much – that's Clark – you kind of disregard him and are dismissive. And when you're around a guy that you're madly in love with – that's Superman – you usually become moronic and your IQ drops about sixty points. You look all gaga. So I brought that to the screen test. Those were the two factors, I'm guessing, that got me the part.

GB: You mentioned that you had read one comic book?
MK: I did read one, after the first audition. I was horrified. It was a comic book that my stepson had, and it was about Lois Lane and the *Daily Planet* staff having a bowling match against these terrible women called 'Women's Libbers'.[17] I was horrified, so I didn't read any others!

GB: Once you were cast in **Superman***, did Richard Donner encourage you to research the comic books or were you working exclusively from the script?*
MK: No, I worked from the script. Donner was terrific. He let everyone do their homework the way they did it. He worked with each person's method. No, he didn't encourage me to read comics at all.

GB: How many Superman films were you originally contracted to make?
MK: Two, I think. I think the original contract was two.

GB: I understand that DC Comics insisted on placing a morality clause in the actors' contracts.
MK: Well, those clauses were very common in my first days as an actress. In all the contracts for all the studios, there was a morality clause – which we all ignored.

GB: Did the clause relate only to things that you did in your private life or to your roles in other projects?
MK: Well, here's what happens when you become famous, which is the weirdest experience that can ever happen to a human being. It's very unsettling – I found it so, anyway – and very strange. Everybody is suddenly peering at you as if you were some monkey in a cage at the zoo. The morality clause applied to you doing nothing that hurt the studio or your image when you were in public. Well, the irony of that is that you're *always* in public. I think the morality clause went back to the 1940s and 50s when they didn't want anyone who was gay to say they were gay, and they didn't want anybody having extramarital affairs. It was kind of a stupid, white Christian American middle-class bit of nonsense. That's why in the Fifties movies, if you notice, the husband and wife were never in the same bed. You couldn't show two people in bed together. The morality clauses were in all of the studios' contracts, and we all thought they were funny. We were all children of the Sixties and we thought they were hilarious.

GB: You mentioned that you thought of Lois behaving one way with Clark and another way with Superman. What other traits did you conceive for the character?
MK: Well, little things within scenes when we'd rehearse. Like when Lois says, 'How big are you? I mean, how tall are you?' – that was actually something that accidentally came out of my mouth at rehearsal, and we kept it. There were several little things like that that happened.

GB: Were there any alternative costumes for Lois Lane than those seen in the film?
MK: No, but I insisted on certain modifications to the costumes. The brilliant costume designer [Yvonne Blake] was very English, and the clothes she chose did not look like clothes and outfits that Americans would put together. I kept saying, 'This is red, white, and blue time. Cut all these patterns off things and make the clothes just straightforward.' So they were less – what's the word I want? Not 'outlandish' – they were simpler than they were initially supposed to be. I just said, 'These colours should be really plain and simple, not high fashion.'

GB: Did you conceive Lois in relation to second-wave feminism?
MK: I didn't think that way, because I *was* a feminist from the beginning of the feminist movement. It seemed to me then, and it does now, that any female who is not a feminist is a masochist, frankly. So I didn't play her on purpose, consciously, as a feminist. I played her as the person Tom Mankiewicz wrote in the script, who was funny, smart and independent.

GB: What was the nature of Mankiewicz's contribution to **Superman***?*
MK: Oh, it was huge. I mean, he made the script. I read the earlier draft by Puzo, the Newmans and Benton, and it didn't very much resemble the draft written by Mankiewicz, who was supposedly the script doctor. But all the wit and the humour and the banter back and forth, which I think made the characters' relationships work, was pure Mank. Now, of course, his uncle was Herman Mankiewicz and his father was Joseph Mankiewicz – they had written 1930s dialogue.[18] If you look back at *Superman*, a lot of the dialogue and the relationships very much resemble those that a young Katharine Hepburn would have had in her romance movies. So there was a wit in *Superman* that was pure Mankiewicz. Every laugh line was Mankiewicz, every double entendre was Mankiewicz. I can't say enough about him. I mean, it wouldn't have worked without him writing it.

GB: Was he a significant presence on the set during shooting?
MK: Well, he was. We started dating. He became my boyfriend after my husband announced that if I was going to go away for a year and make a movie he would divorce me. So that part of the plan worked! [Laughs.] And I got Mank instead, which was just

delightful. And after our romance ended, we stayed really close friends and talked all the time. His death just shattered me. He was wonderful.

GB: You have often said that Donner is very insightful about acting.
MK: Yes. It's a very weird job, acting. Most people think what you're doing is lying, and in fact what you're doing is trying to tell the truth as much as humanly possible so that the emotional reality of the character is honest. So, when you're sad, you're sad, when you're up and silly, you try to make yourself up and silly – that sort of thing. So, you do your homework first: you learn your lines, know why you're in a scene, what it is you want when you come into the scene, what you have to do to get it and what hurdles you have to overcome to get it. All that stuff is your homework at night. But once you're on the set, all that homework has to be put away in the part of your brain that makes it automatically playable. Acting is like Zen Buddhism. And then you have to skate honestly through whatever emotions you think are going on. It's like getting on skis and going right down from the top of a steep hill, not quite knowing what bump in the snow is going to come up. So you plan out what you want to do, and then you get on the film set and hope, as you point the skis down, that you can stay up all the way to the bottom. You hope that you can manoeuvre your way through the moguls, so to speak. And Dick Donner always made that very easy. He's a very funny guy, Donner. He's big on practical jokes. So when things got tense, he'd do some kind of practical joke and then we'd all be roaring hysterically, and then go at it again.

GB: Some of the tension on the set arose out of a clash of acting styles. You once told me that your acting method involves a lot of spontaneity whereas Christopher Reeve disliked improvisation. How were the two of you able to reconcile your contrasting approaches?
MK: Well, sometimes we didn't. We had fights. And if I'd improvised something, Chris would cut take and say, 'You can't do that.' And I'd yell, 'Shut up! Don't tell me how to act. This is your first movie and my tenth!' Donner could defuse the tension like nobody I'd ever seen. He was really wonderful. One of the most irritating things about Christopher was that he tried to tell everybody what to do all the time. Even on the first Superman movie, when he'd done no film before. That's one of the reasons I'd say, 'Shut up, Chris! You don't know what you're talking about.' And he was not very thoughtful of other people's feelings. He could be a real asshole, frankly. But over time, Chris became much easier to work with.

GB: You didn't meet Marlon Brando on the set of **Superman**, *did you?*
MK: No. I had directed *The Missouri Breaks* [making-of] production movie [in 1976], and I met him then and adored him. But I didn't see him in London [on *Superman*]. I think he'd left, in fact, by the time I got there. In *Missouri Breaks*, he had his lines written all over the set. In the garden scene, he had them on the fence post. Sometimes the other

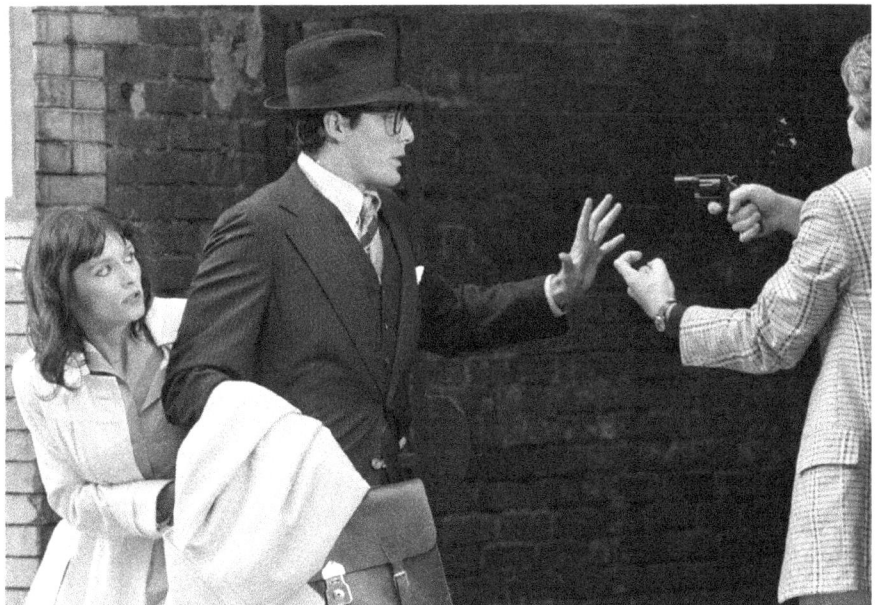

Figure 3: Margot Kidder and Christopher Reeve filming a scene from *Superman* in New York City. Photo: AP/REX/Shutterstock.

actors would actually wear a mask for his close-up with his lines written on them. The only one who refused was the young ingénue [Kathleen Lloyd]. She said, 'I'm not going to do that; if you want to act with me, you have to learn your lines.' So he did. So it was clear he *could* learn them. But there was something about him that was mesmerizing. I don't know what it is, what that quality is, I really don't. I was very sad not to see him on *Superman*. I loved him. He was hilariously funny and very warm and tender and loving and smart. He could have people eating out of his hand, you know?

GB: One of the key scenes in Superman is the interview scene on Lois's balcony. Tonally, it's perfectly pitched, but I imagine it might have been difficult finding the correct balance of humour, romance and drama. Did this scene involve much rehearsal?
MK: It was actually one of my audition scenes. You know, the actual scene on the balcony was easy to act. It was flying off the balcony that was a fucking nightmare! We landed in the walls and in the bushes. It was the first time anyone had tried doing flying effects using blue screen, and it was done the way they did Peter Pan in the olden days: there was a wheel with a cord that winches you up, and you shot forward. The guy operating my wheel, Derek, was a little drunk and he tended to land me in all the wrong spots. Oh,

it was a nightmare. I can't remember how many takes we did of that scene. Chris and I slammed together in mid-air and then hit the wall. It was just crazy.

GB: Besides the flying and action scenes, were there other scenes in **Superman** *that posed a particular challenge?*
MK: Well, it wasn't fun getting crushed in an earthquake. [Laughs.] The challenges were all physical. And Donner made them funny.

GB: The balcony scene segues into the flying sequence over Metropolis, during which you recite a poem ('Can You Read My Mind?'). How did this recital come about?
MK: I was originally supposed to sing it. Donner said, 'You're singing it. You're going to see John Williams.' So I said, 'Okay' and I went over to John Williams' house. And of course there's an Oscar on every mantelpiece. So I was a bit intimidated. He played the theme for me a couple of times, and said, 'Now sing it.' After three or four times, he called Donner and said, 'She can't sing.' Donner said, 'I don't care, she's going to sing it. She's got a distinct voice.' I was filming *Amityville Horror* in New Jersey between the first and second Superman films, and I got the call that I was to come and sing. I went to New York on the day I wasn't filming, and went into the studio and started singing. I started singing louder and they didn't say anything, so I thought I was doing great. I got louder and louder. I could see John Williams rolling his eyes. Finally, Donner came up and said, 'How about you *talk* it?'

GB: Donner was right, though, you do have a distinctive voice.
MK: Oh, thank you. It's because when I was young I smoked too much!

GB: Had you done any singing before, professionally?
MK: Oh God, no. I did a play called *Sylvia* and I had to sing – God, I can't remember the song. And one night, the director came backstage and said to me, 'Even Beethoven couldn't figure out what notes you sang tonight.'

GB: In the 1970s, you were very much a part of the New Hollywood community documented by Peter Biskind (1998) and others.
MK: Yeah, that was before *Superman*.

GB: Did your peers from that group offer any opinions or advice about your involvement in **Superman***?*
MK: By then I was living in Montana and had a little kid. Everything had changed. No, nobody ever gave me any advice. We didn't do that. We didn't give each other advice, really. I'd left that scene by that stage. And I'd acted lots.

GB: Did you have much interaction with the Salkinds and Spengler during the making of Superman?
MK: Unfortunately I had a little, yeah. Disgraceful people.

GB: You still feel that way about them?
MK: I have a moral code that I was brought up with that they broke daily, and I have no time for them. They were liars, they were thieves, they were laundering money, they fired the man [Donner] who made them rich. I'm sorry, you don't do that sort of thing.

GB: The producers replaced Donner with Richard Lester, who completed the filming of Superman II. *Did Lester have a different concept of Lois Lane than Donner?*
MK: Well, Lester didn't *have* a concept of Lois. If you've done a part for a while, directors don't talk to you about what they think your character is. In fact, nowadays most directors don't talk to actors at all, because they don't know anything about acting. [Replacing Donner with Lester] was a silly thing for the Salkinds to do. But they owed Lester so much money. You know the real story of why Lester did it, right?

GB: The producers owed him money from the Musketeers movies?
MK: Yeah, they hadn't paid him. He'd sued them in seven different countries, because they owned passports for seven countries. And so if he sued them in Mexico and won, the company would be found to be worth one paso. And so he did get a vacant lot in Mexico and he sued them in Switzerland, where they were, I guess, living. He couldn't win. So they finally said, 'Well, if you finish this movie [*Superman II*], we'll pay you all that we owe you and a percentage of the profits.' And he said 'Yes,' I would think quite reluctantly, not knowing how much it meant to Donner. So they fired Donner. Now, all that was really left to shoot between Chris and I was two scenes. But then the Directors Guild said, 'Wait a minute: you can't have Lester direct two scenes and have his credit on the movie. He has to have directed at least 50 per cent of the scenes and they have to be brand new scenes.' Oh, dear! So we had to change things. They wrote some very awful new scenes for Chris and I, like the one with his hand going into the fire and all that crap.[19] And then we shot the scenes really fast. So when you look at the Richard Donner cut of *Superman II*, it's *so* much better than the *Superman II* that was released in theatres. It's night and day.

GB: Which scenes in the Donner cut are you particularly proud of?
MK: Well, the main one is how I find out that Clark Kent is Superman. And that whole beginning scene of Donner's cut: the scenes in the office with Clark Kent, Lois jumping out of the window and landing on the fruit cart – all of that stuff. *All* of it. That footage sat in a vault for twenty or thirty years. Then this thing called Comic Con became such a phenomenon. Every time I did a 'question and answer' session with the fans at Comic

Con, I'd tell the story of how the Salkinds fired Donner. And all these fan letters came pouring into Warner Brothers, and then Donner got the chance to re-cut *Superman II*. Oh my God, his version was so much better.

GB: How did Lester's directorial approach differ from that of Donner?
MK: Well, I was close to Donner, so we'd joke together and he'd get me in a certain mood. I found Richard Lester, although he was a very clever and very funny guy, to be a little bit unreachable and aloof. But a director doesn't determine how your character turns out. They determine how the scene turns out. *You're* the person driving the car behind your character. And so you know how you've got to do certain things. If the director didn't agree with those things as you displayed them in rehearsal, then you had to sit down and talk. If he thought, however, 'Oh, look what this person has brought to this character' and it works for him, he left it. In my experience, there are not long discussions between you and a director about who your character is.

GB: So in terms of characterization, there were no real hurdles that you had to navigate?
MK: No. You know, there's that adage in movies: you can make a bad movie from a good script but you can't make a good movie from a bad script. And we had a really, really good script, and we went by the script. I mean, it was a blueprint that was just fabulous, so we went along with that and it was great.

GB: In Superman *and* Superman II, *Gene Hackman and Terence Stamp created colourful, memorable villains.*
MK: Oh my God, they were wonderful. Gene is such a brilliant actor. I would sit mesmerized by what he was doing and forget I was in the scene. There would be a pause and Donner would shout, 'Kidder!' and I'd say 'Oh my God!' because I was just mesmerized by watching how wonderfully Gene worked. He was brilliant, a genius guy. Gene did a different thing in every take. And Terence Stamp and I got to be buddies and I just adored him. Unlike Chris, he didn't stay in character. He was very funny and warm and terrific. He's a very smart guy; you could have interesting conversations with him. But we didn't have any real interaction in the scenes. I mean, the villains were real comic-book characters, whereas Chris and I were [playing] real people.

GB: You were conscious of working in a different style than Hackman and Stamp?
MK: Yeah, there were two different styles of acting. I think when you read the script, the difference is clear. I mean, I don't know how either Terence or Gene could have played it differently. They couldn't really play anything else.

GB: Your role in Superman III *is essentially a cameo.*
MK: I wasn't on the set much in *Superman III*, because I'd said to *Time Out* magazine in

London that the producers were beneath contempt as human beings, and the magazine put it on the cover.[20] So the producers wanted me out of that movie. I was glad I was not in it. I had twelve lines. One line was, 'Oh Clark.'

GB: And Superman IV? *Director Sidney J. Furie tends to get written out of the accounts of that film. It is as though Christopher Reeve held the dominant creative role and Furie was only the nominal director.*
MK: Oh, I love Sidney. I know Sidney from another movie *[Pride of Lions]*; he is a pet, he's just a doll. Not much is said about him because by then Chris, of course, thought he knew *everything* as he'd done three Superman films and tended to just push everybody around.

GB: I imagine that over the years your feelings about being associated with Superman *have fluctuated….*
MK: Well, yes, I'm an old woman now! [Laughs.]

GB: Was there ever a time when it was frustrating to be identified so closely with Superman?
MK: Not really, because I made a real point of playing different characters in every movie I did.

GB: During shooting, you reportedly believed that Superman *would be a flop. At what point did you realize the film would be successful?*
MK: Well, I didn't know how great it was going to be until we were at the premiere in Washington, DC. I was stunned at how good it was. Just stunned. And I cried all the way through the flying sequence. I was amazed.

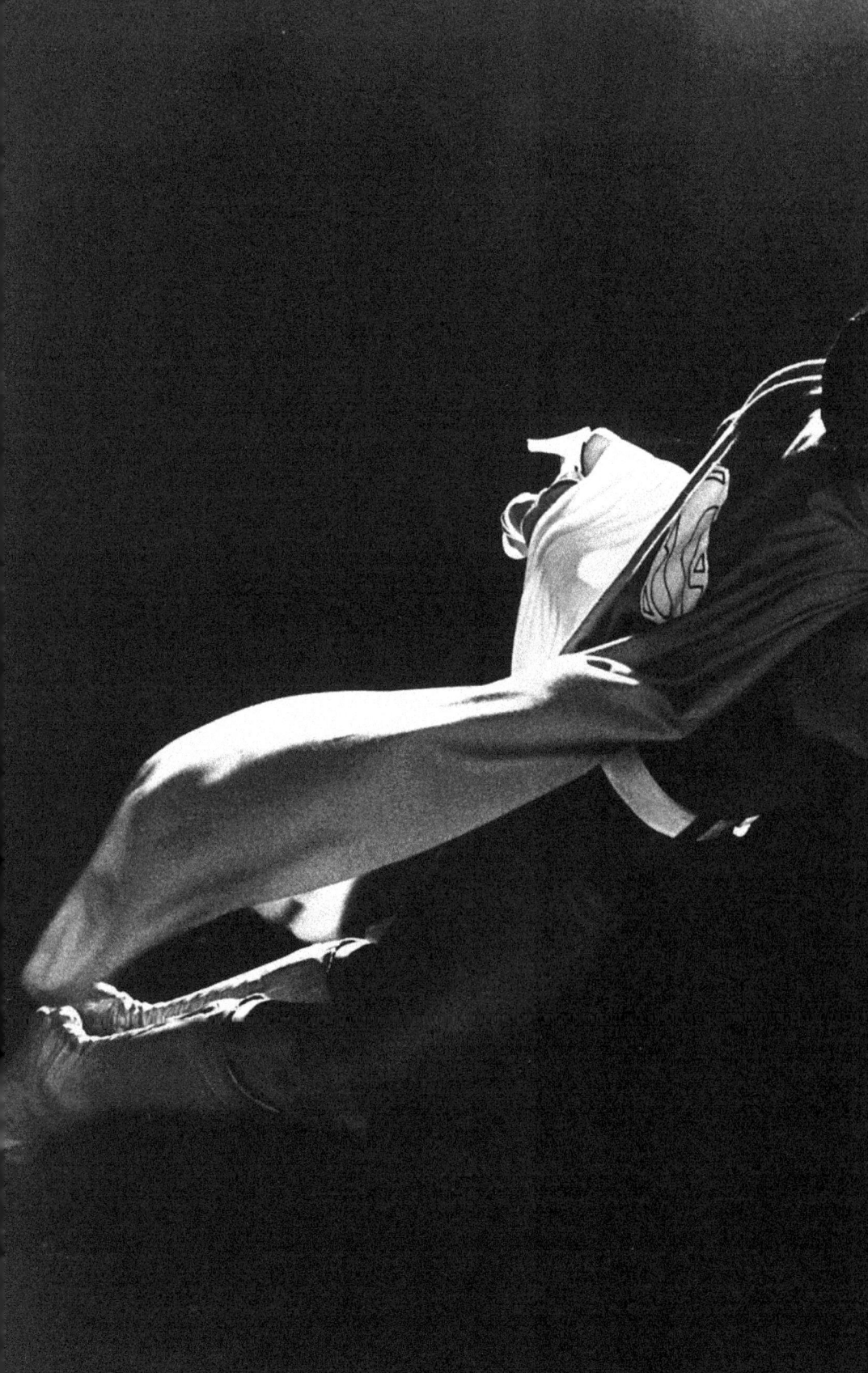

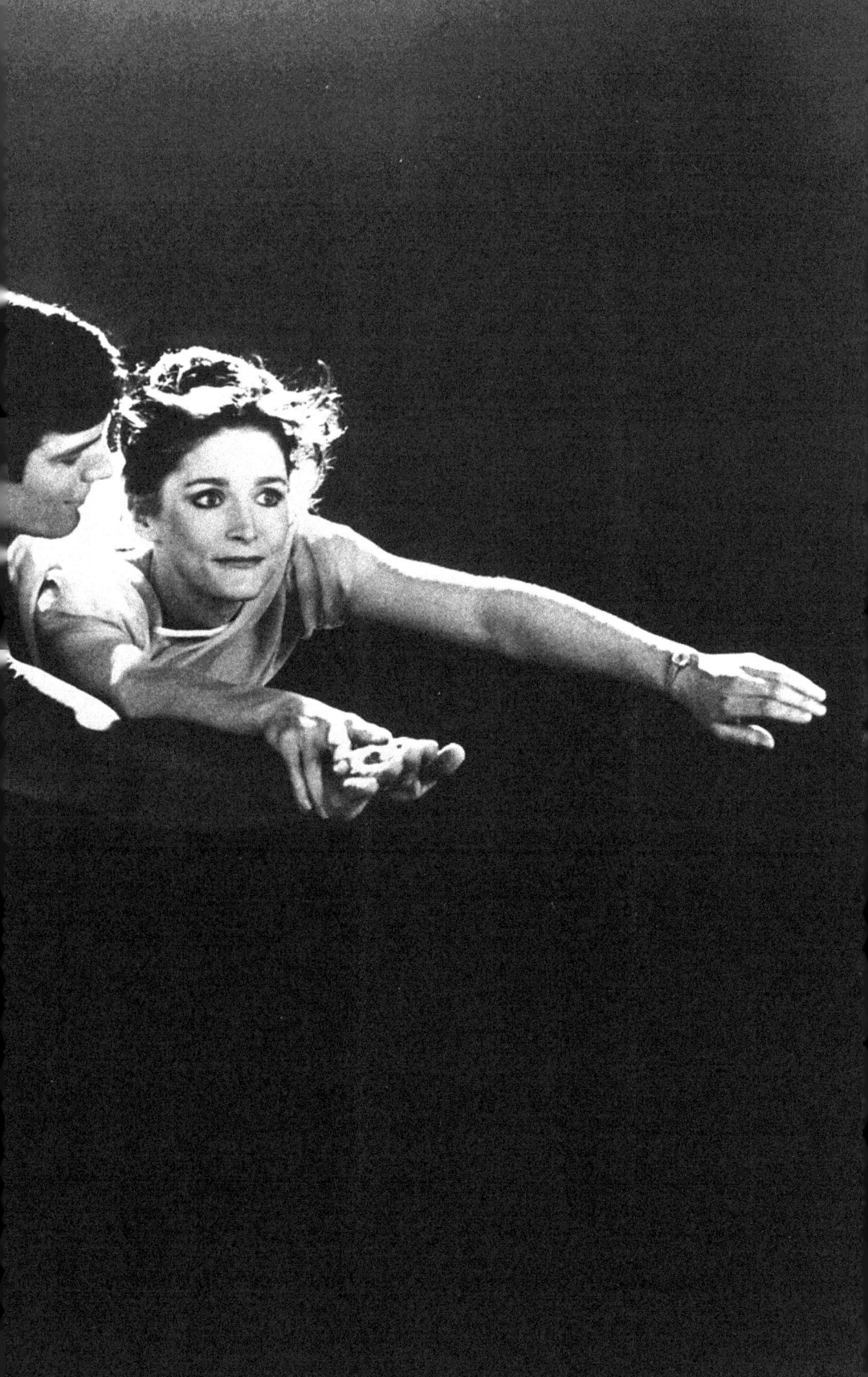

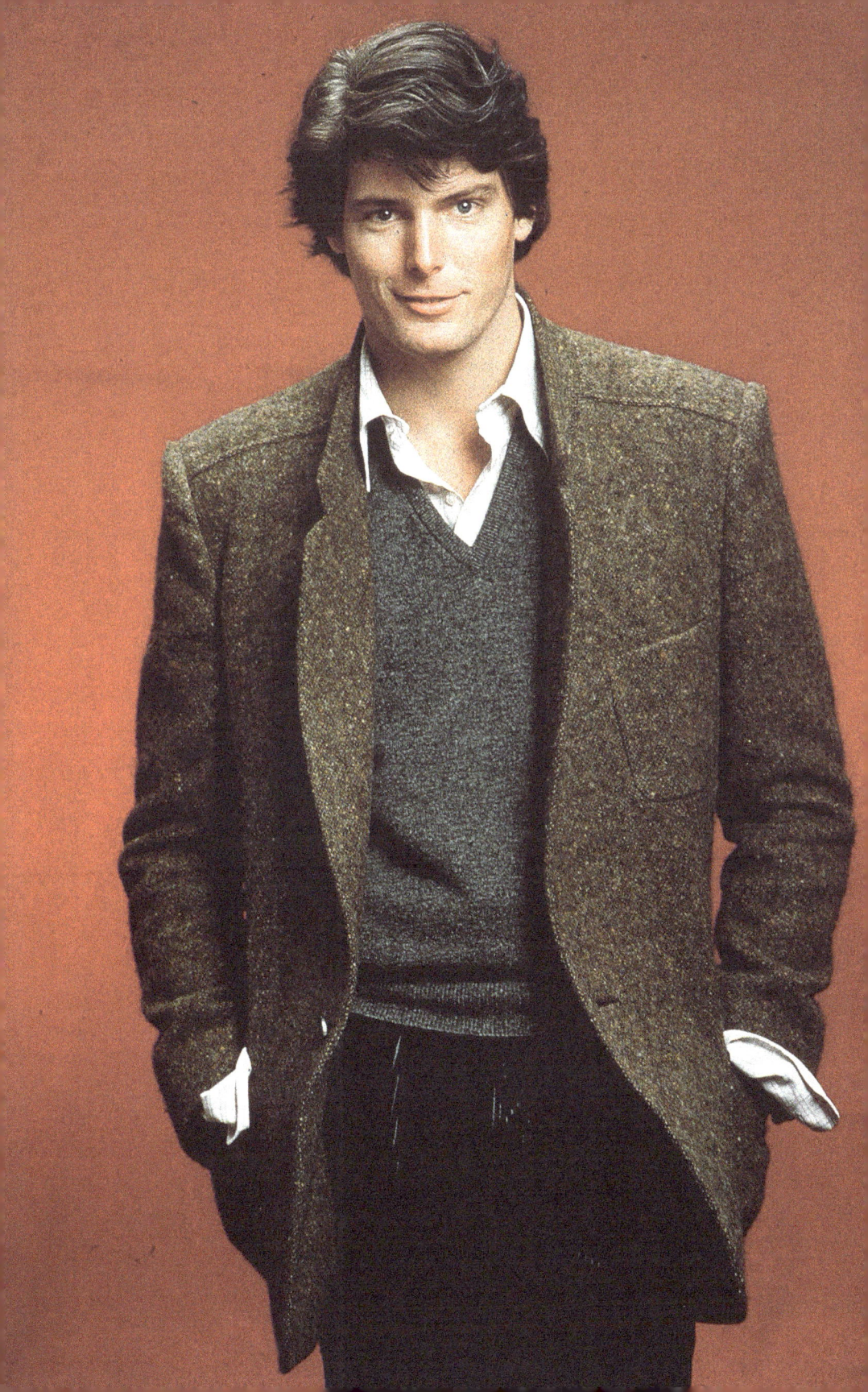

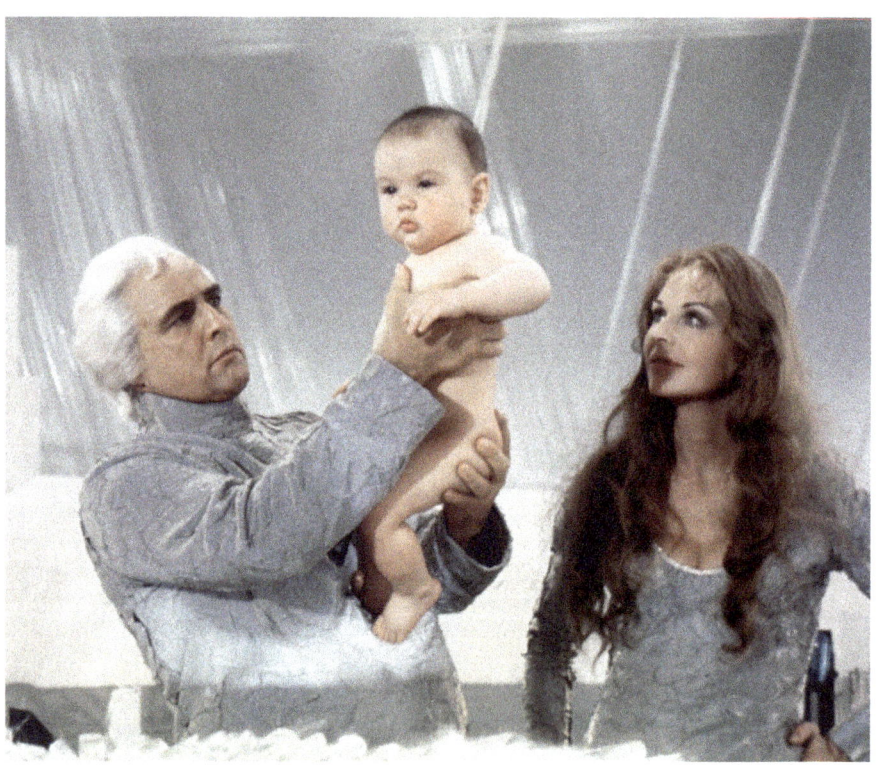

Previous page: Figure 4: Newcomer Christopher Reeve proved ideally cast as Superman and Clark Kent. Photo: Kobal/REX/Shutterstock.

Above: Figure 5: Jor-El (Marlon Brando) and Lara (Susannah York) bid farewell to their infant son, Kal-El (Lee Quigley). Photo: Warner Bros/DC Comics/Kobal/REX/Shutterstock.

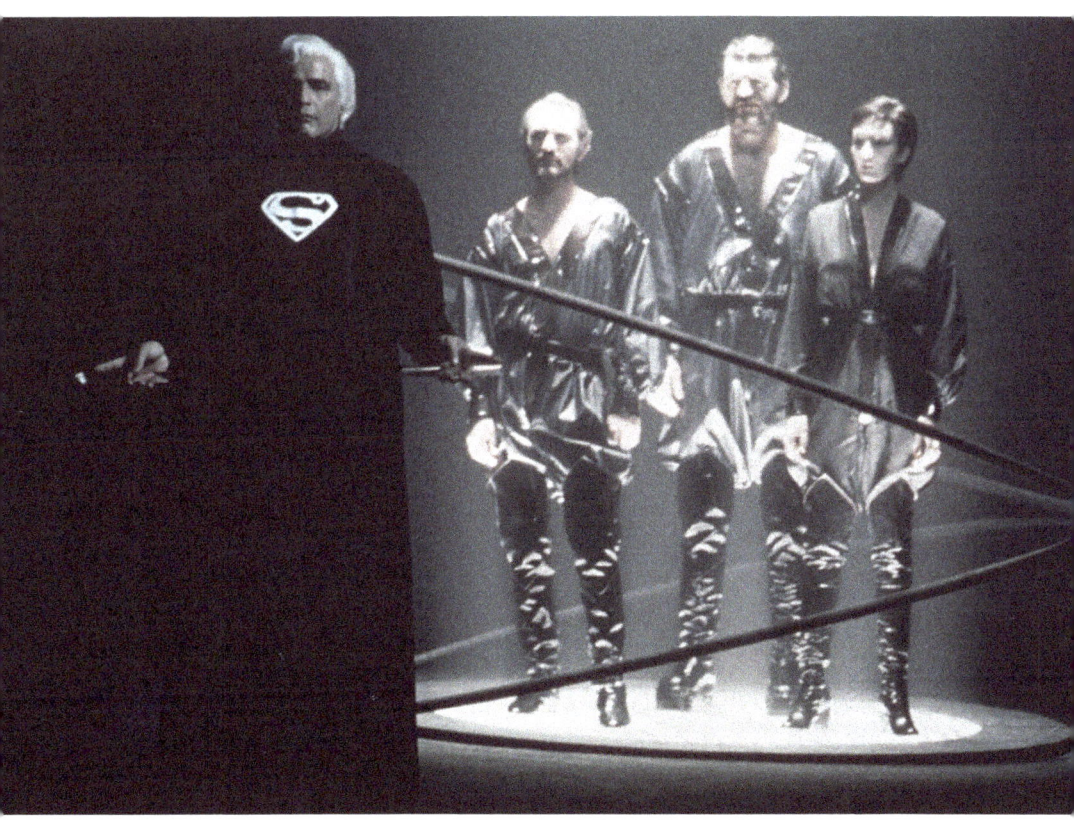

Figure 6: Jor-El (Marlon Brando) banishes General Zod (Terence Stamp), Non (Jack O'Halloran), and Ursa (Sarah Douglas) to the dystopian Phantom Zone. Photo: Warner Bros/DC Comics/Kobal/REX/Shutterstock.

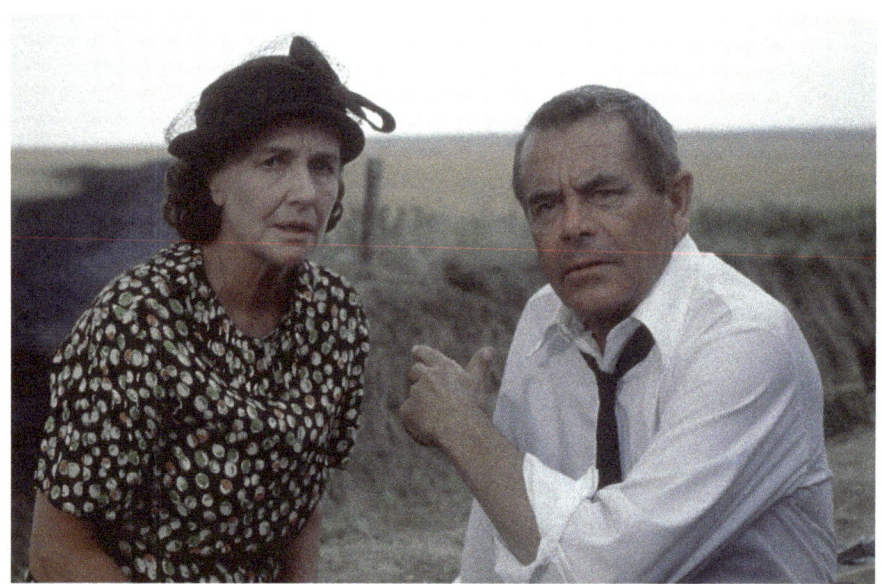

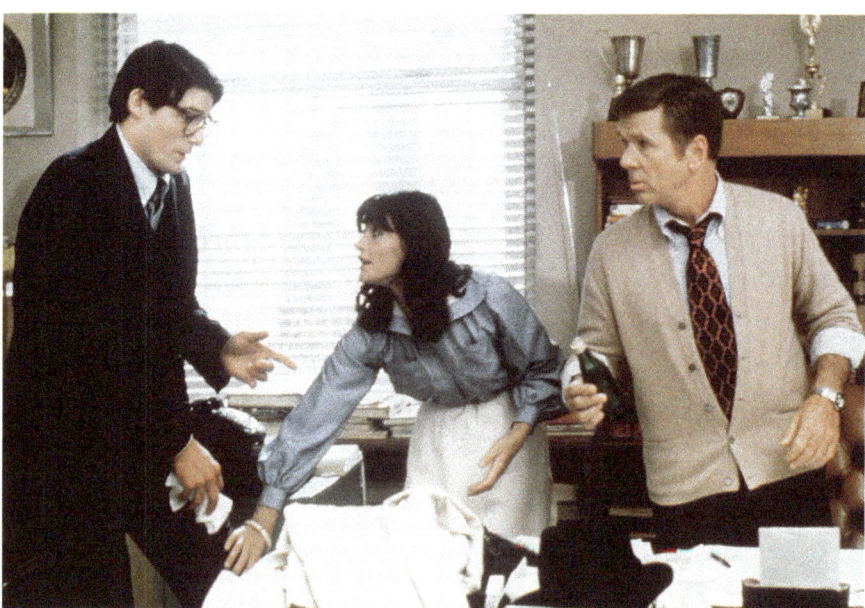

Figure 7: Phyllis Thaxter and Glenn Ford as Kal-El's adoptive parents on Earth. Photo: Warner Bros/DC Comics/Kobal/REX/Shutterstock.

Figure 8: Arriving at the Metropolis *Daily Planet*, mild-mannered reporter Clark Kent (Christopher Reeve) meets Lois Lane (Margot Kidder) and Perry White (Jackie Cooper). Photo: Warner Bros/Kobal/REX/Shutterstock.

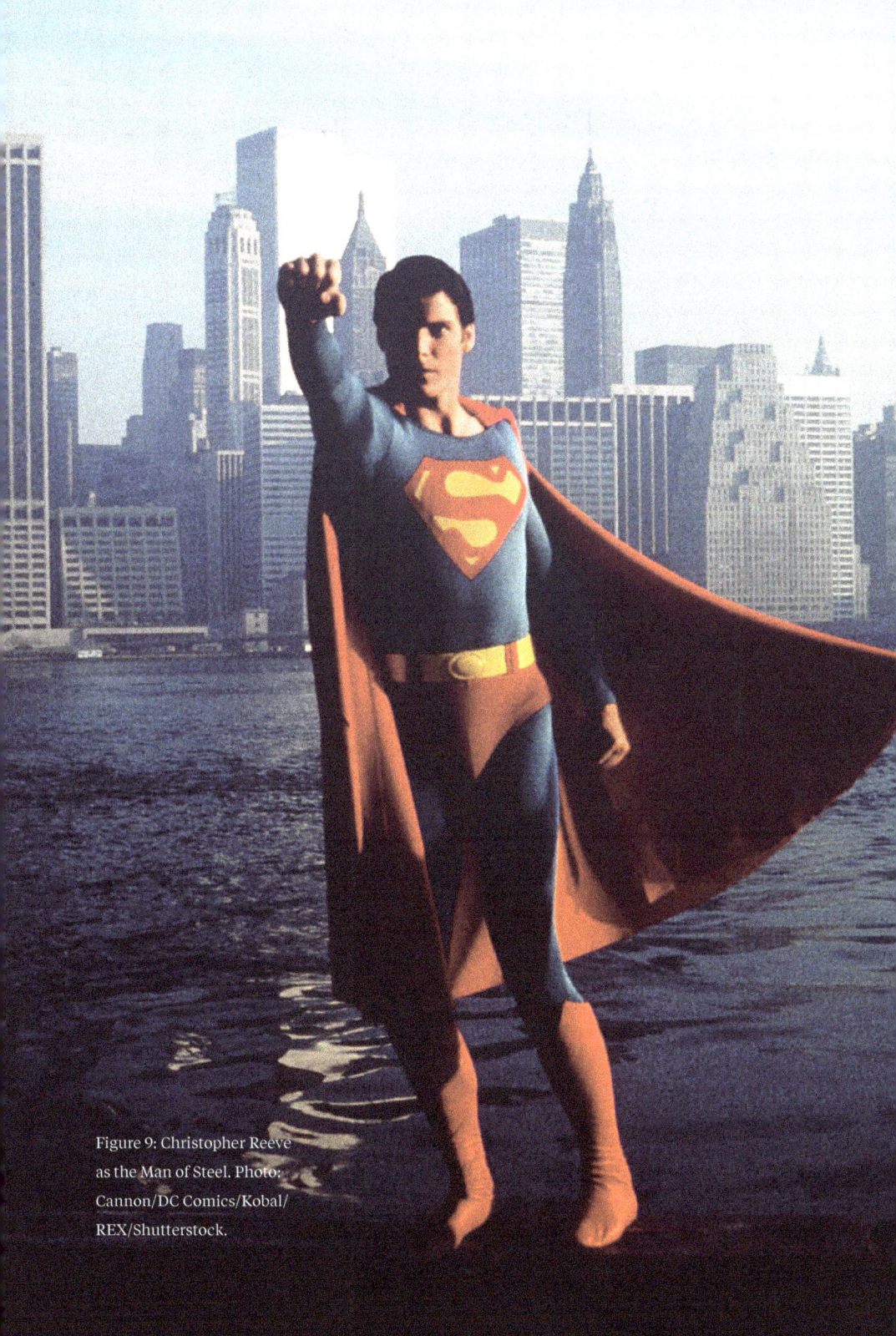

Figure 9: Christopher Reeve as the Man of Steel. Photo: Cannon/DC Comics/Kobal/REX/Shutterstock.

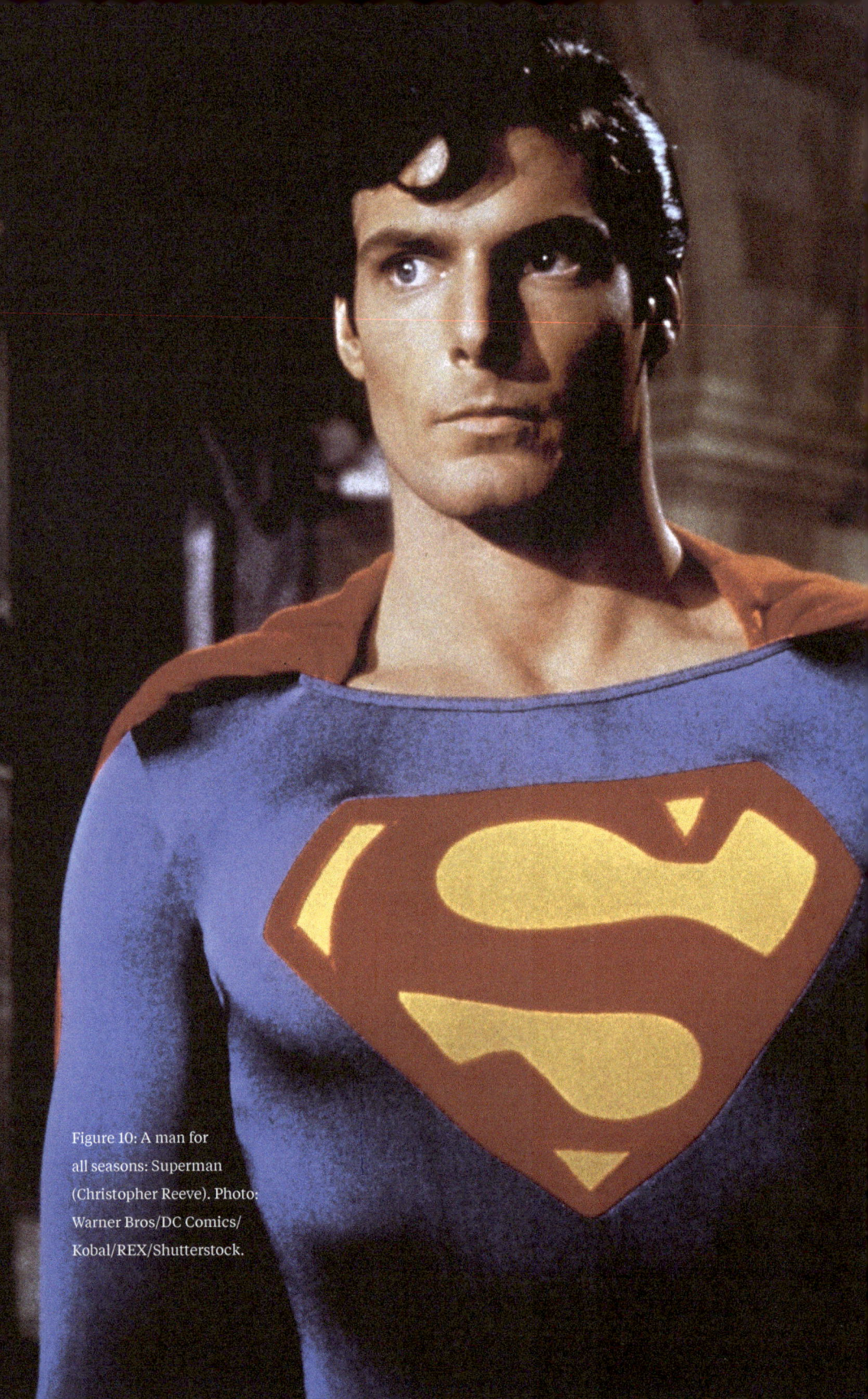

Figure 10: A man for all seasons: Superman (Christopher Reeve). Photo: Warner Bros/DC Comics/Kobal/REX/Shutterstock.

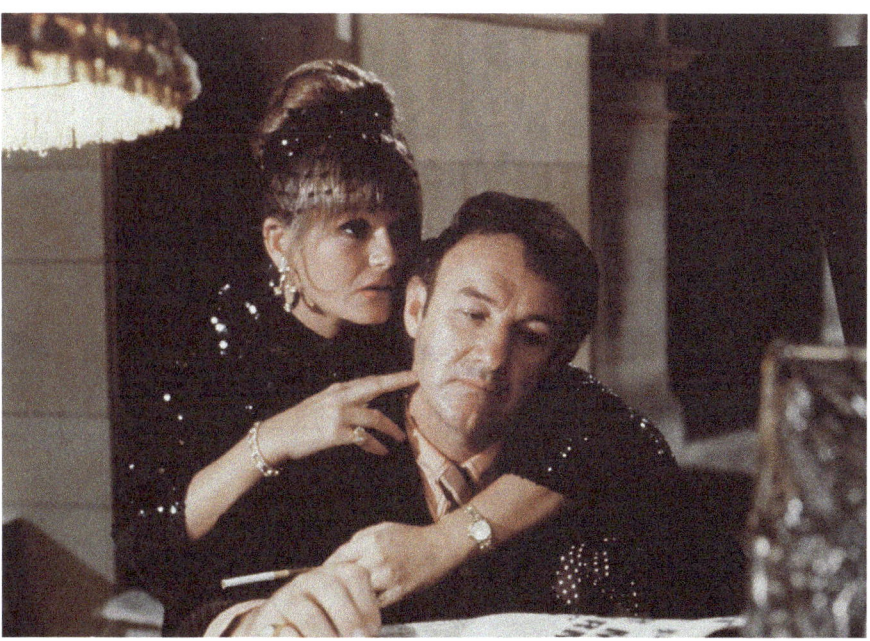

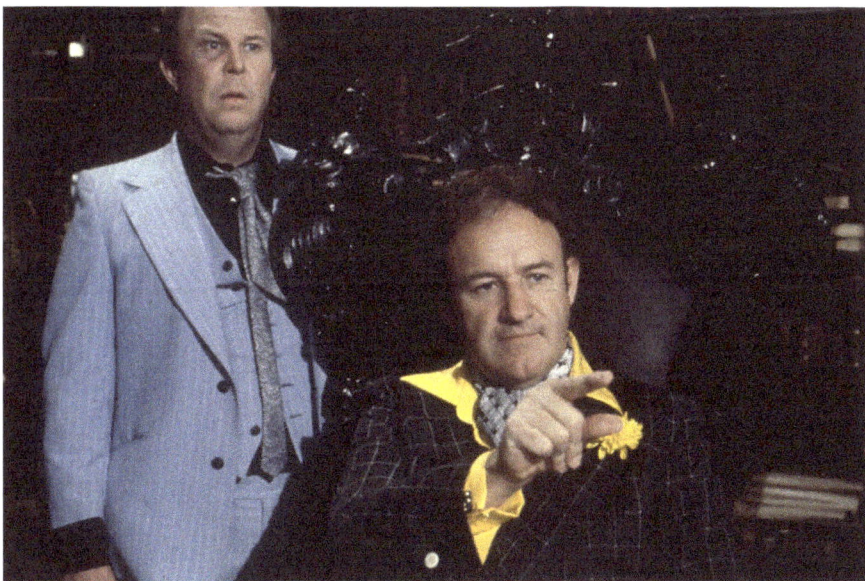

Figure 11: Lex Luthor (Gene Hackman) and Eve Teschmacher (Valerie Perrine) plot Superman's downfall. Photo: Warner Bros/DC Comics/Kobal/REX/Shutterstock.

Figure 12: Ned Beatty as the buffoonish Otis, underling of Gene Hackman's Lex Luthor. Photo: Warner Bros/DC Comics/Kobal/REX/Shutterstock.

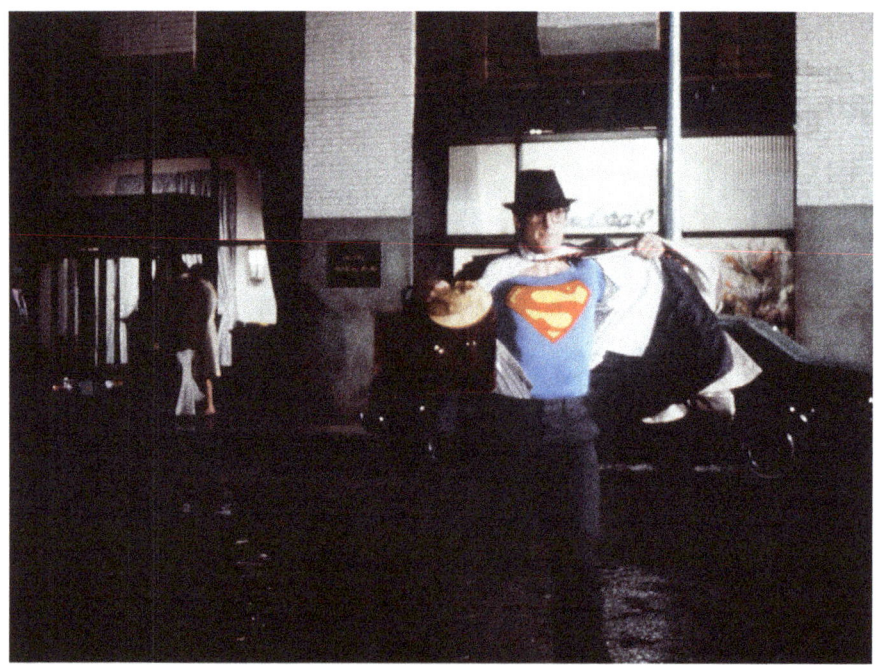

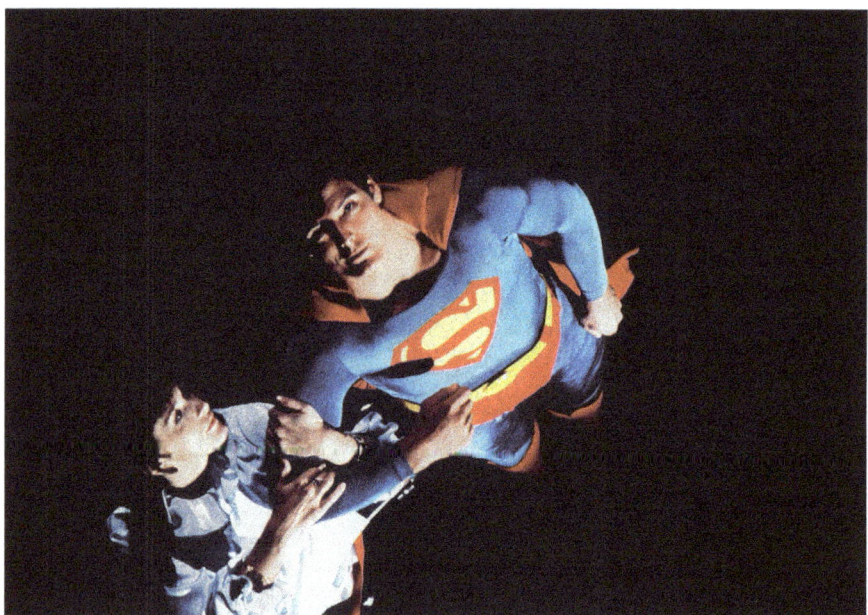

Figure 13: Clark Kent (Christopher Reeve) to the rescue. Photo: Warner Bros/Kobal/REX/Shutterstock.
Figure 14: "Can you read my mind?" Lois Lane (Margot Kidder) and Superman (Christopher Reeve) take flight. Photo: Warner Bros/DC Comics/Kobal/REX/Shutterstock.

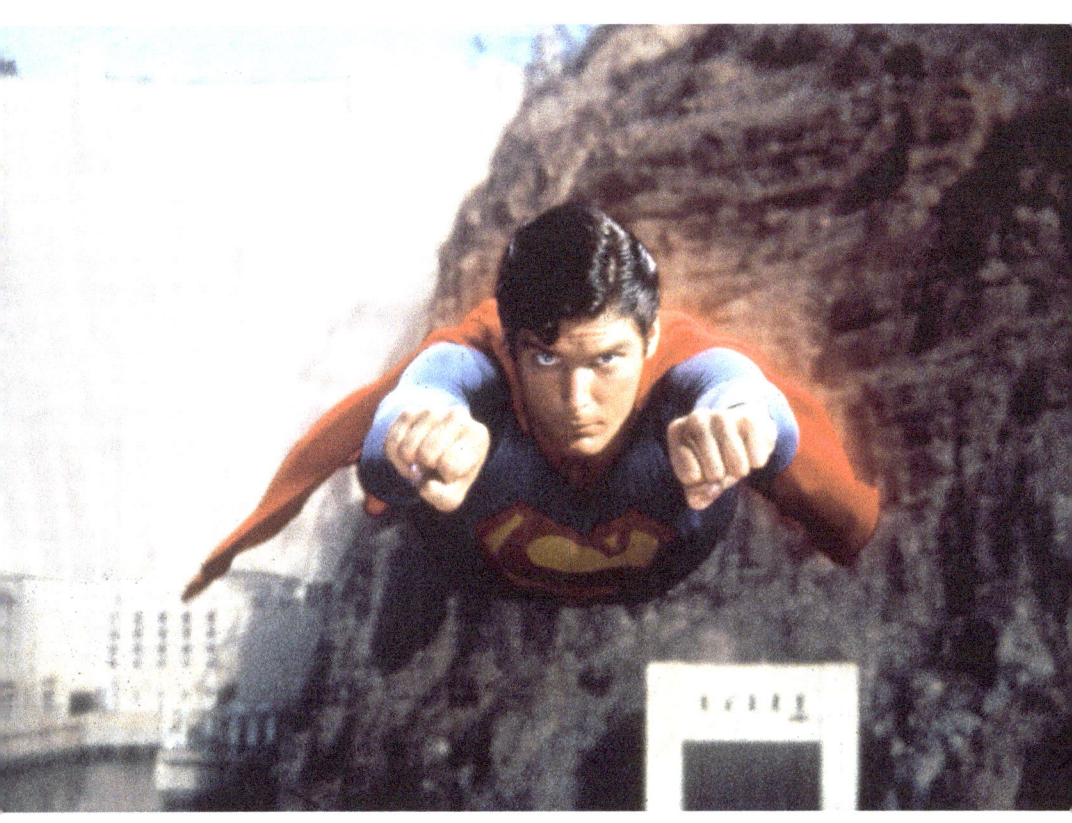

Figure 15: Faster than a speeding bullet: Christopher Reeve as Superman. Photo: Moviestore/REX/Shutterstock.

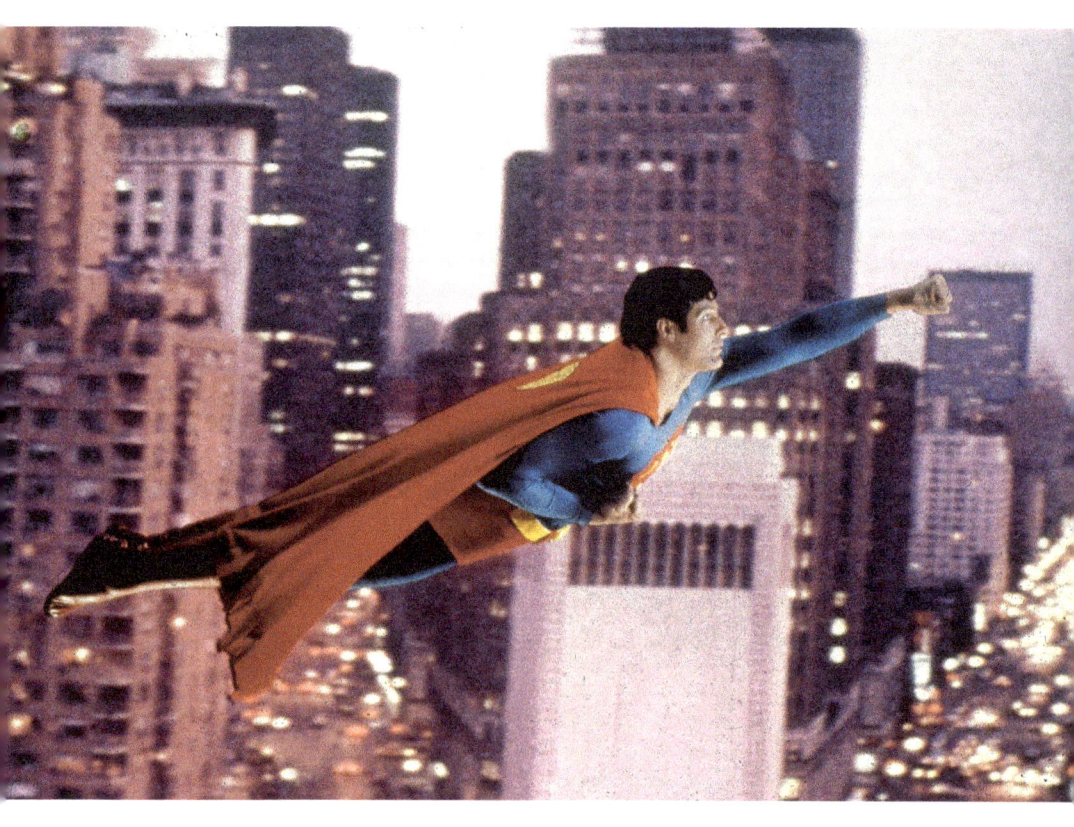

Figure 16: Superman (Christopher Reeve) patrols Metropolis. Photo: Moviestore/REX/Shutterstock.

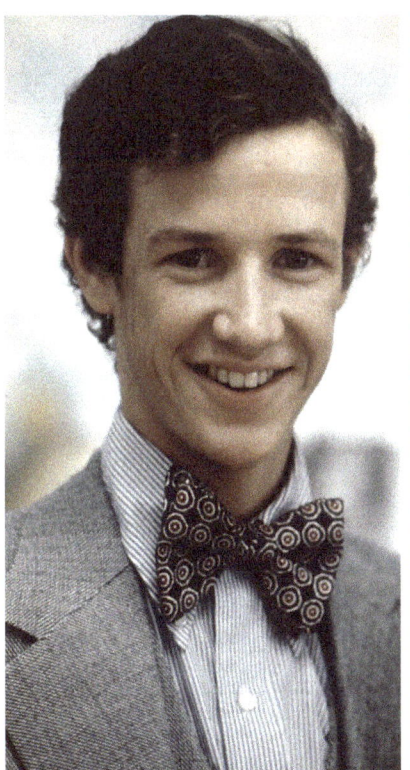 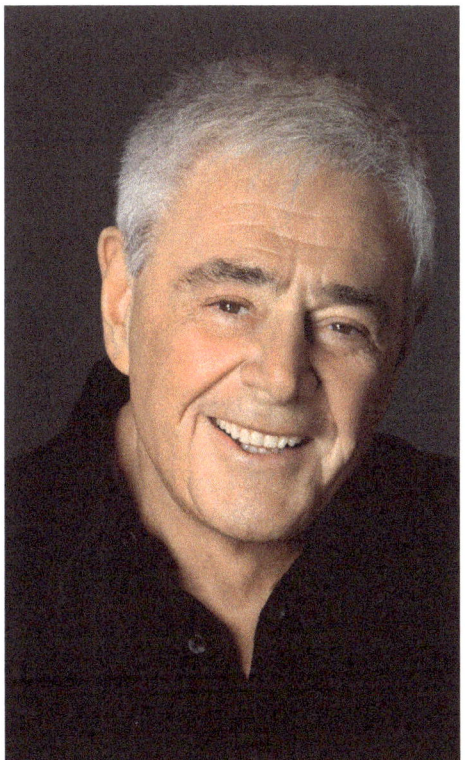

Figure 17: Marc McClure as Jimmy Olsen, *Daily Planet* photographer. Photo: Warner Bros/DC Comics/Kobal/REX/Shutterstock.

Figure 18: *Superman* director Richard Donner. Photo: The Donner Company.

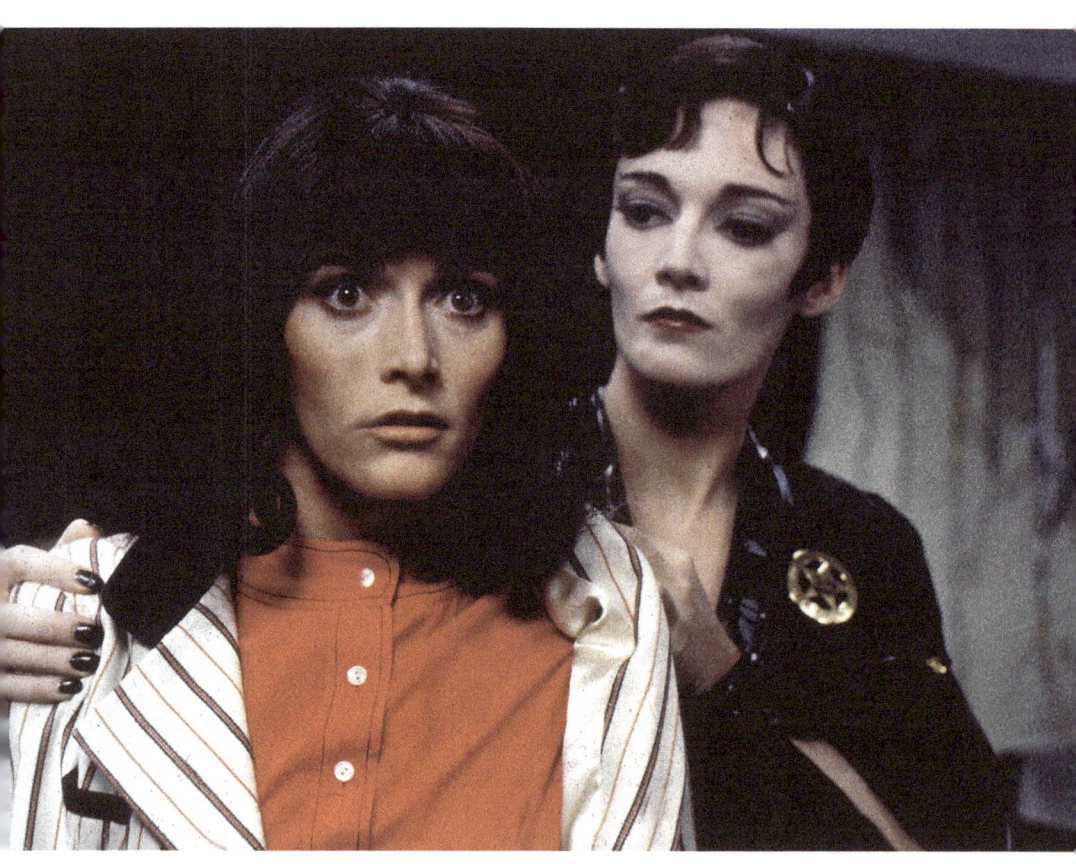

Figure 19: Ursa (Sarah Douglas) gets to grips with Lois Lane (Margot Kidder) in *Superman II* (Richard Lester, 1980). Photo: Moviestore/REX/Shutterstock.

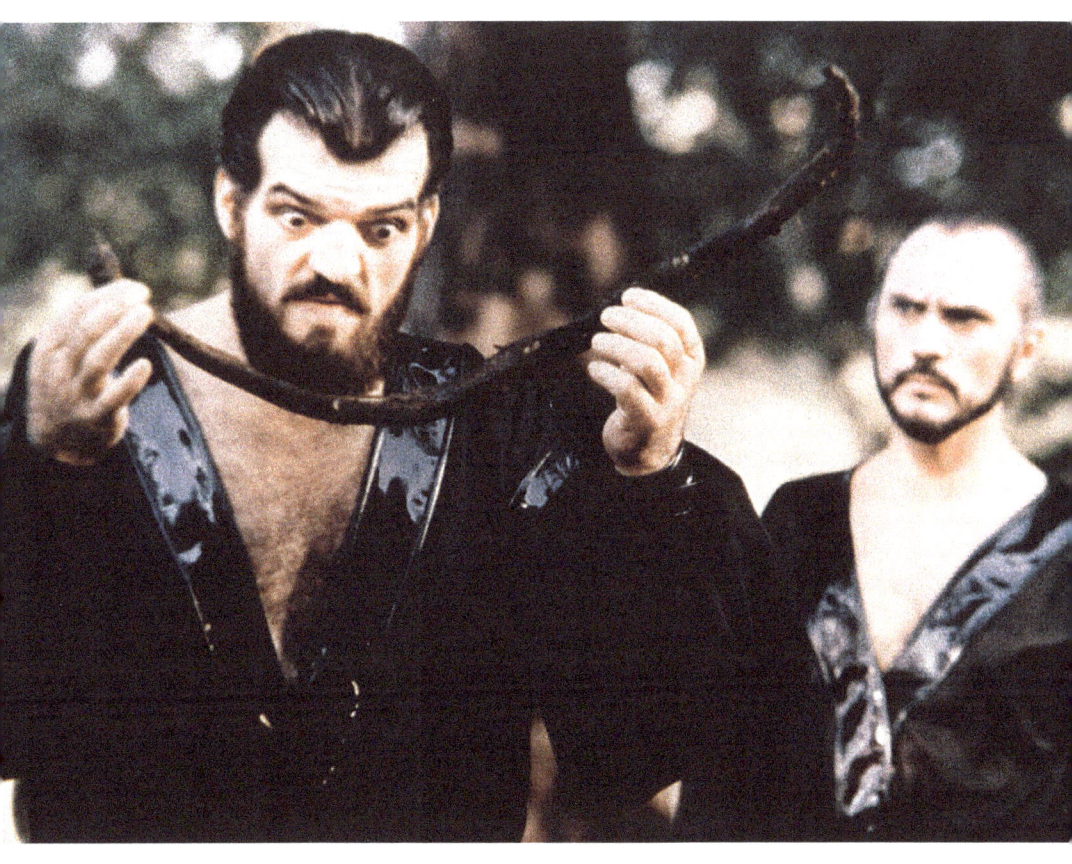

Figure 20: *Superman II*: Kryptonian villain Non (Jack O'Halloran) masters his heat vision, as Terence Stamp's General Zod looks on. Photo: Warner Bros/DC Comics/Kobal/REX/Shutterstock.

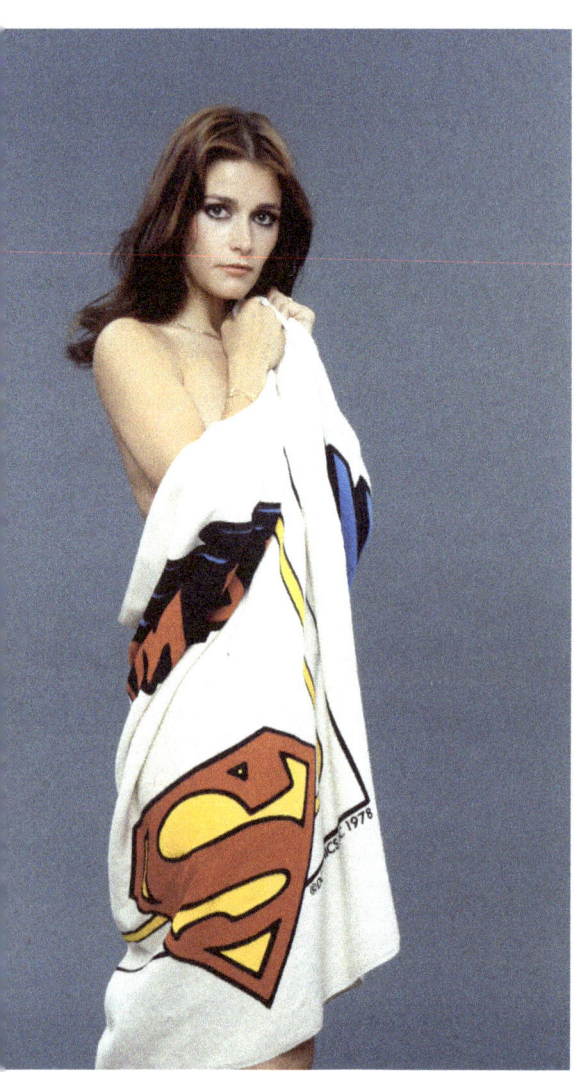
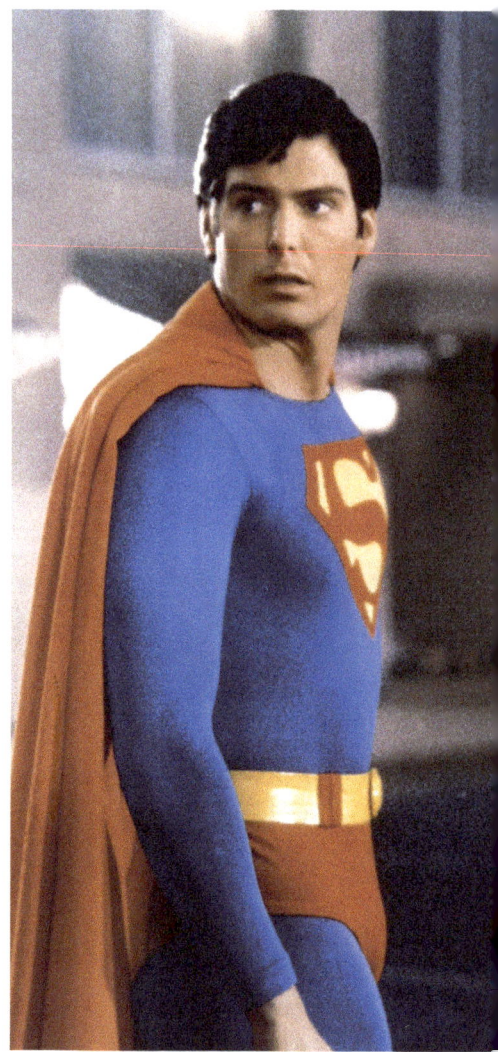

Figure 21: Margot Kidder, a Lois Lane for the 1970s. Photo: Marc Sennett/REX/Shutterstock.

Figure 22: In *Superman* and its sequels, Christopher Reeve portrayed the eponymous hero as both 'a friend' and 'a gentleman'. Photo: Warner Bros/DC Comics/Kobal/REX/Shutterstock.

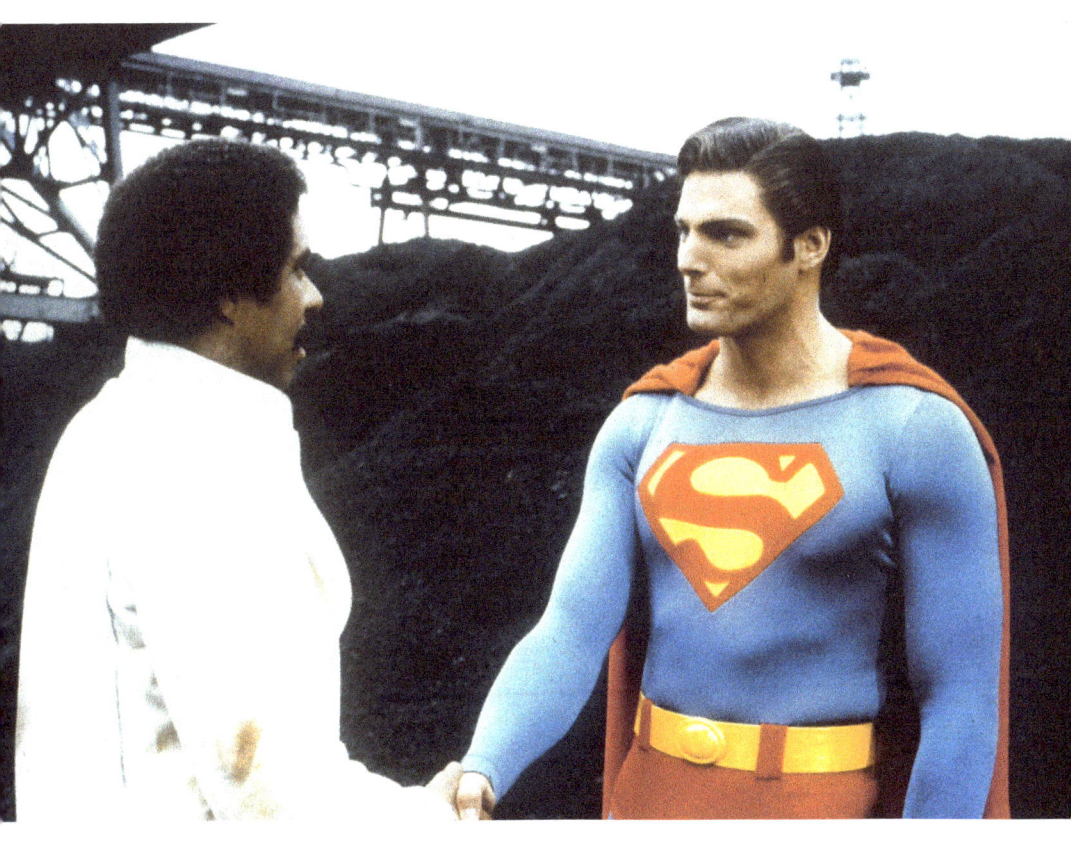

Figure 23: Superman (Christopher Reeve) befriends computer genius Gus Gorman (Richard Pryor) in Richard Lester's *Superman III* (1983). Photo: Moviestore/REX/Shutterstock.

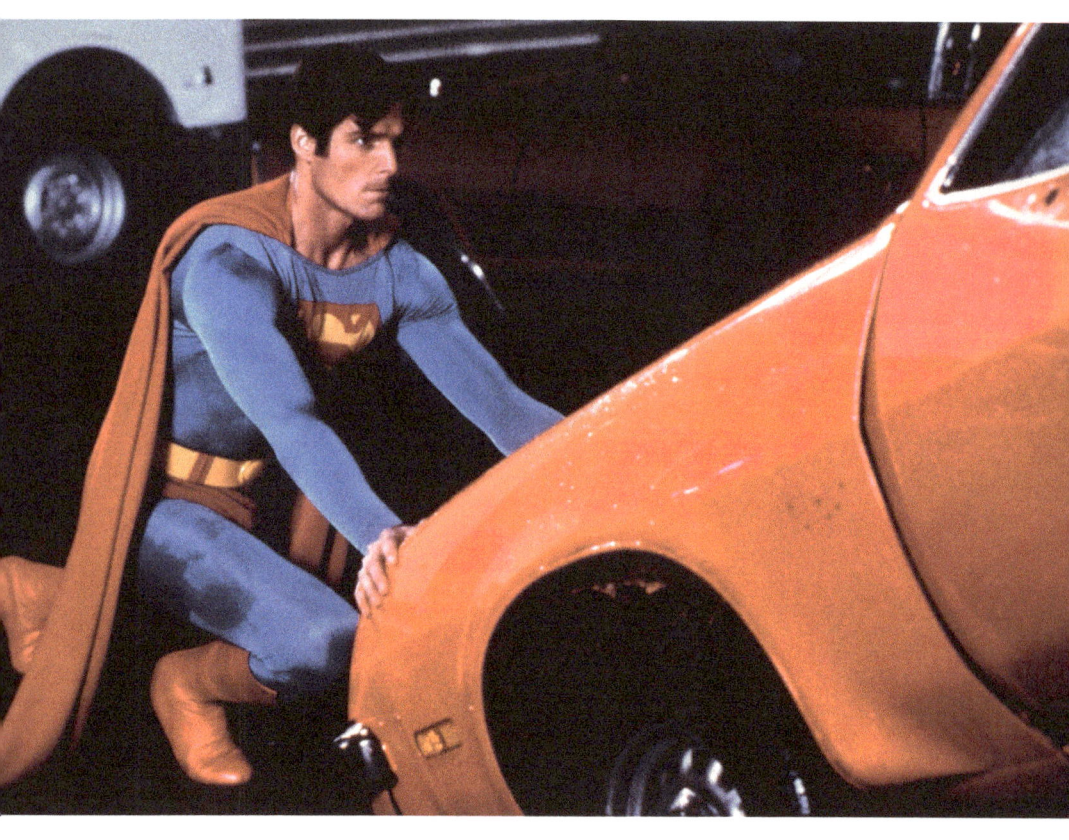

Figure 24: Christopher Reeve's finely-judged performance could not rescue *Superman IV* (1987) from box-office failure and critical derision. Photo: Cannon/DC Comics/Kobal/REX/Shutterstock.

"There was a lot of magic on Superman. Dick Donner was a very big ingredient in that great-tasting pie. When they fired Donner, everything changed. All of a sudden, the story of Superman: The Movie made a big right-hand turn."

MARC MCCLURE

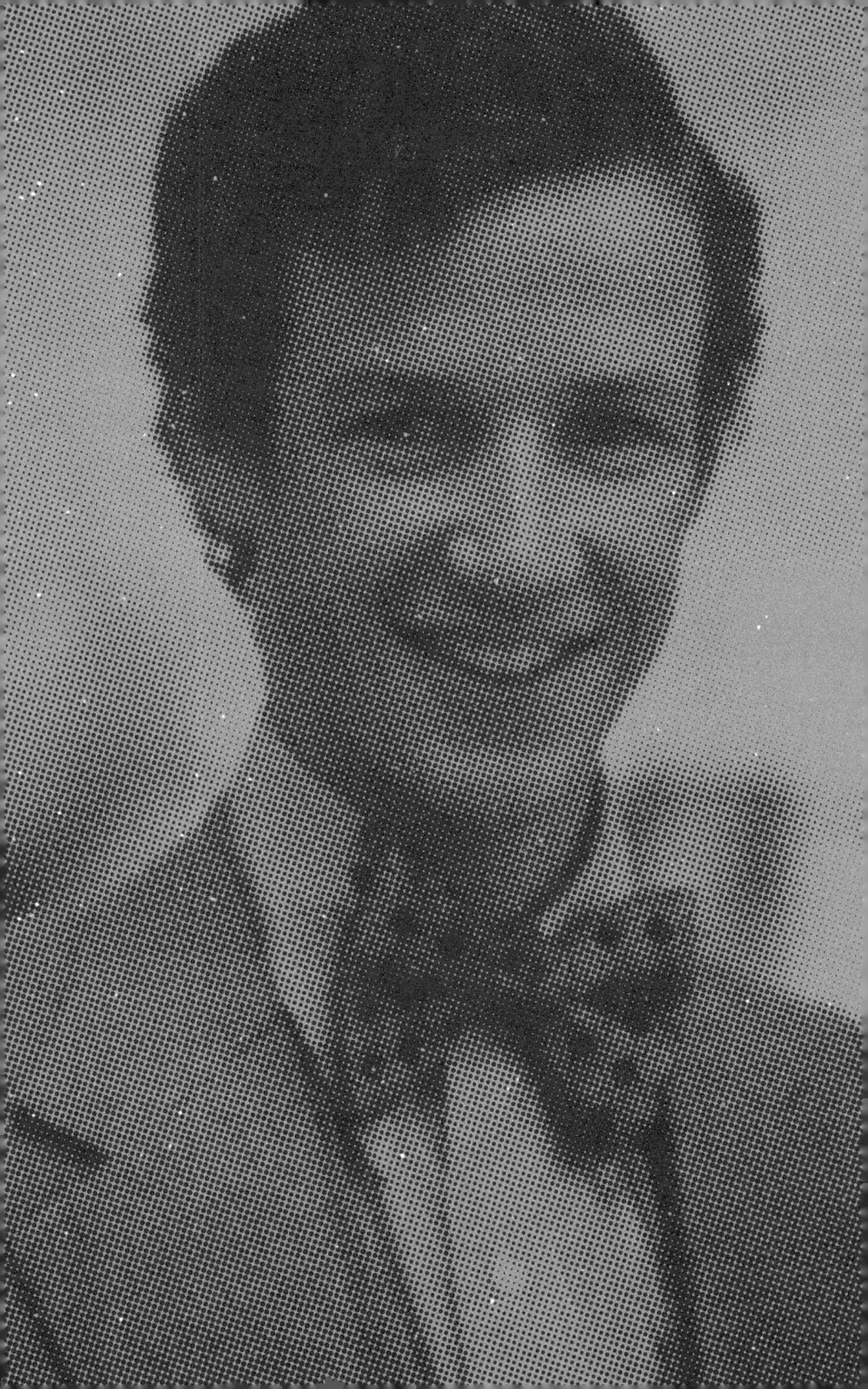

MARC MCCLURE
JIMMY OLSEN

Gary Bettinson: Could you describe the process of being cast in Superman*?*
Marc McClure: Well, I went to [casting agent] Lynn Stalmaster's office where Dick Donner and Tom Mankiewicz were. I was 20 years old, and I was living on a house boat in Marina Del Rey. So I went into the interview and Donner asked what I was doing. I said, 'Well, I'm living on a house boat and I'm cleaning the bottom of boats.' He had always wanted to live on a boat. We just started talking about boats for the whole interview. We didn't really talk about *Superman*. Finally after about fifteen minutes he just said, 'Thanks for coming in,' and I said, 'Yeah, great, thanks,' and headed towards the door. And he asked me if I knew who Jimmy Olsen was. I said, 'Golly, Mr Kent.' And he laughed, and I left. And I *did* know who Jimmy Olsen was, from watching Jack Larson's portrayal in the black-and-white TV show.[21] Anyway, after the meeting, I would keep hearing stories about *Superman* making progress, the casting of Marlon Brando, Christopher Reeve and so on. And I thought to myself, 'Well, that opportunity has gone; it's probably not going to happen.' Finally the agent called and said, 'They want to see you again.' So I went back to Lynn Stalmaster's office, and Donner said, 'We just wanted to remember what you look like.' And about a week later I was off to London to play the role of Jimmy Olsen. So I never had to read for the part. That's one of those things where the universe looks after you, and you just find yourself in the right place at the right time.

GB: At what stage in the casting process were you hired? You say that Reeve and Brando had already been cast...
MM: Yeah, everybody was already working. Right when I first arrived in London, I was driven to Shepperton studios, which was where they had built the Fortress of Solitude set. I walk onto the sound stage just as Donner yells 'Action', and they fly Chris from one end of the set to the other. And everybody starts clapping after that take. I wasn't quite sure what was happening, but that was the first time they filmed Chris flying and realized they were going to make this thing work.

GB: You mentioned that you were familiar with Jack Larson's portrayal of Jimmy Olsen. Once you were cast in **Superman***, did you revisit episodes from the 1950s* **Adventures of Superman** *series?*

MM: No, I already knew them. I finally met Jack Larson after I got done filming *Superman: The Movie*. I went in search of him; I just wanted to meet him. He was living in a Frank Lloyd Wright house off Sunset Boulevard. He was a great guy, and he still looked like Jimmy Olsen. He would tell me stories about being cast in the Superman television series. Jack had been signed to a certain studio; he was part of their stable of actors. The executives told him, 'Hey, we want you to play this Jimmy Olsen role, but it's probably going to be real quick – you'll be done with it in no time.' Well, when he got that role in the Superman television series, it just turned his world upside down. George Reeves too. Noel Neill. All of them. Jack was a pretty serious cat. He really enjoyed his acting.

GB: What character traits did you devise for Jimmy Olsen?

MM: The most important thing about Jimmy is his energy and his naivety towards everything. He reacts before really thinking things through, which is the brilliance of Jimmy. He'll find himself in trouble quicker than he should. Jimmy Olsen has such great energy and he's such an honest person. He is just very true to himself.

GB: Did your costume and make-up help to inform your portrayal?

MM: Appearance-wise, the make-up department dyed my hair a little red and put freckles on me. The main thing, though, was the bowtie. The bowtie was a great symbol for Jimmy Olsen. The bowtie kind of made Jimmy who he really wanted to be. It really, I think, made him proud to put that bowtie on; that was his identity. The Chief – Perry White – wears a bowtie too, and Jimmy emulates the Chief. I think that was a conscious thing that Donner wanted: as far as when it comes to the Chief, Jimmy wants to please him as much as he can.

GB: How else did Richard Donner shape your portrayal?

MM: Well, I'm sure you've heard it many a time: Donner was just a real amazing person. The way he let us work and the way he got it done. There was a scene in *Superman*, set in the *Daily Planet* office, where the Chief sends me out to get him tea. They were filming my close-up first. Jackie Cooper was supposed to say, 'Don't call me Chief' – that's how the line was written in the script. But he accidentally said, 'Don't call me sugar.' And my reaction to that was: 'Okay, sugar.' I just reacted to it when the camera was on me. When Donner turned the camera around to get Jackie's close-up, he had Jackie say the 'Chief' line but he also had him say the 'sugar' line. And they ended up using the 'sugar' line in the movie. That was the magic of that film. Donner was really open to accident.

GB: What was Jackie Cooper's attitude towards the project?
MM: I think he had been acting since he was 4 or 5 years old doing vaudeville. This guy was never out of the business in his lifetime up to then. That's all he did, was be an actor. That's all he knew. He was flawless. He was prepared, he was funny. You know, Jackie Cooper came into the project after Keenan Wynn had a heart attack.[22] Jackie came in at the last second. Jackie was so good; his energy, as the Chief, is unbelievable.

GB: Did you relate easily to Donner's vision of verisimilitude?
MM: Yeah, I've always been an actor who is all about believability. Believability was probably the most important part of the Superman project: to make the audience believe that all of these people on screen are real. In all of my films, I just try to be as honest as I can. But it all comes back to Donner. We all just created our characters and we tried to make them as believable as we could. When I first arrived in London, I was ready to go; I was shake-and-bake. I *was* Jimmy Olsen. I think I locked into it pretty good; I didn't really have to think too much about it. Donner's directing was fantastic. But I think I just captured Jimmy from the start. You know, there was a lot of magic on the Superman project. Dick Donner was a very big ingredient in that great-tasting pie. It's a hard thing to describe how good he was to us and how much he did protect us. The producers were hanging around the set, and Donner was trying to do his thing. They were, I believe, trying to interrupt him with either ideas or instructions to 'hurry up.' Donner was fired after the premiere of *Superman: The Movie*, before we got to finish the last part of *Superman II*. Such a mistake. When they fired Donner, everything changed. It certainly would have been interesting if the Salkinds had left him alone and let him be. We'll never know what might have been. Why the Salkinds fired him after the success of *Superman* is mind-boggling. All of a sudden, the story of *Superman: The Movie* made a big right-hand turn.

GB: I take it that you prefer the Donner cut of **Superman II**?
MM: Oh yeah! Are you kidding? There is no comparison. When Richard Lester came in to take over, I didn't beef about it much because I was a young kid and I was having a great time. But I did realize that this new guy in town was very, very different from Donner. And I wasn't quite sure how things were going to work out until I saw the film. But, you know, you can look at the Donner cut and you can look at Lester's cut and just see two different people trying to tell a story. What a difference. From somebody who really cares and loves the comics and Superman, and understands the respect it deserves, to a guy who just comes in and makes money. You don't have to be a rocket scientist to figure out which one is going to be better.

GB: You said that Donner protected the cast members. Do you mean that he shielded you from his disputes with the Salkinds and Spengler?
MM: Oh, yeah. He dealt with them. I think Tom Mankiewicz also dealt with them quite

a bit. Donner, I think, at one point said to the producers, 'You guys have got to stay away from me. You can't keep coming up to me every day saying that I've got to work faster.' Donner was working on five sound stages at once. He was running from sound stage to sound stage, trying to get this film ready for a Christmas release. Donner and Tom Mankiewicz were super tight, and both those guys worked harder than anybody. Tom was on set almost every day. And like I say, he was the guy that kept the Salkinds away from Donner. That was one of his jobs, besides working on the script.

GB: Speaking of the script, did you ever see Mario Puzo's draft of **Superman***?*
MM: Yeah, I still have the Mario script. It's gigantic – a very thick script, because it was parts *I* and *II* together. It was much different from Mankiewicz's version, but it was all kind of there. There was much more detail in Puzo's draft. It was almost like Puzo was writing a book instead of a script, where the details of things were really elaborate. Tom Mankiewicz's script was much more formulated to an actual script.

GB: Did Richard Lester bring to the sequel his own interpretation of Jimmy Olsen?
MM: To tell you the truth, I don't know if he even knew who Jimmy Olsen was. That's a curious question. I don't know if he even knew who Jimmy Olsen was as a character.

GB: But he didn't, for example, instruct you to play the character differently than you had been doing under Donner's direction?
MM: No, not at all. With Lester, it was kind of up to me, and I tried to push for a little bit more believability. Unfortunately, it has to be that the director is going to have the final say; he's going to have the edit, and you could tell that things were not in click. We were losing the believability of the fantasy that we had created in *Superman: The Movie*. Margie [Kidder] was tough. She actually created a lot of – let's call it 'vibe' – on the set, where she wasn't really happy being there, and that would kind of spread around. So it wasn't just me; everybody was feeling that this particular project was a little bit off the rails. One of Lester's main goals was to finish *Superman II* as quickly as he could. So he shot with three cameras. And there really wasn't much connection on the set after Donner left. I'm sure the crew would tell you the same story. I know it didn't make a lot of people happy, that's for sure. Chris probably would have been the only guy to demand that Donner be brought back, but I don't know if Chris was feeling that he was in a position to do that. Looking back, I believe if Chris had made a stand, Donner probably would have been brought back. But with his contract, maybe he really couldn't. Maybe his lawyers said, 'Look, you've got to just forge forward and do this; you don't really have a voice in it.' My understanding is that the Salkinds owed Lester money from a previous project, *The Three Musketeers*, and said, 'Look, if you finish *Superman II*, we'll pay you.' And he said, 'Whatever it takes.' That's what I've heard, and whether that's true or not I don't know.

GB: I understand that Christopher Reeve asked you to stay in character while you were on set.

MM: Looking back, I understand where he was coming from. I just think he was trying to understand the world and the characters. I'm not quite sure how in tune Christopher was with Superman when he got the job. I'm not sure if he was into the TV series or the comics. I think that's where it came from: he literally was just trying to understand who Jimmy was through me.

GB: You worked with Reeve on four Superman films. Did his approach to the work change over the years?

MM: He became more involved in the scripts. He also became a little bit more involved in the direction of it. I continued to be a worker bee. But Chris definitely had more say in what was going on. I don't know if he ever called Donner and said, 'Hey, how about you coming back and doing *Superman IV*?' I don't know if that ever happened. Sidney J. Furie ended up directing *Superman IV*, and, once again, he really wasn't the right guy for that job. Jeannot Szwarc directed *Supergirl*, Richard Lester directed *Superman III* – unfortunately those guys were not the right guys for Superman. When it comes to Superman, who's the kid in the room? Who's the comic-book geek? Who really cares about Superman? So far, Donner's the only guy I know.

GB: Speaking of the Superman sequels, how many instalments did your original contract commit you to make?

MM: I was signed for seven Superman movies. I'm not quite sure what the other actors' contracts read. I think Donner was signed for seven movies also, I do believe.

GB: When you were making **Superman: The Movie***, could you tell that the scenes were effective? Or, given that much of the film depended on special effects, were you not sure whether it would all come together?*

MM: Yeah, I wasn't sure. It was pretty early on in my career. Donner always invited us all to come and watch the dailies of what we had shot the day before. I attended some of those. But I find watching myself on film a little bit confusing. For me, it's hard to see myself and be judgmental. So I kind of ended up not going to those things. But what I saw was really good. You really knew that you were in a first-class section. You had the feeling that this was going to be good. It was happening right in front of your eyes.

GB: And the first time you saw the completed film was at the premiere in Washington, DC?

MM: Yes, the very first time. I think it was the first viewing for most of us. It was great. I've been lucky enough to be in some pretty solid films, like *Back to the Future* and *Apollo 13*. *Back to the Future* was one of those films where you didn't really know if it would work, because even reading the script was confusing! But when we saw the first screening of *Back to the Future*, it got a standing ovation from the cast and crew. We realized that we were part of something special. Same deal with *Superman: The Movie*. After the premiere in Washington, DC, everybody realized that the movie was so spiritually hopeful and fantastic. Christopher Reeve was the new face in town, Margie was looking fantastic, and everybody was at their peak. And then we got on a plane and flew back from Washington to London and, as soon as we got back to London, Donner was gone. It was that immediate. Margie *loved* Donner. His departure did not sit well with that cowgirl.

GB: Superman: The Movie *marks its 40th anniversary in 2018. To what do you attribute the film's success and longevity?*
MM: It really comes down to Chris. I remember going to lunch with him, and he'd eat two huge plates of food and then he'd go work out. I mean, he really became big during the making of that film. That's all him in that outfit. There were no layers, like they have these days. That was him, in a pretty skintight outfit. I'm happy for Christopher Reeve's lifetime. That is one thing that I got from this whole endeavour. I really appreciate that guy. I appreciate that moment in time. In life, you don't realize the importance of the moments you're in. But when you say 40 years, it's kind of unbelievable because I remember it like it was yesterday; it was such a powerful part of my life. In 2000, Margie and I went to Metropolis Illinois, which is a town that is all Superman. We were signing autographs and we looked at each other almost at the same time, and it was this shared realization of how important this film is to so many people. The Superman project was beyond any kind of normal project that an actor could do. I go to watch all these new comic-book movies these days, and I'm really rooting for Superman. I want to go into the movie theatre and I want the torch to be passed. To be honest, I haven't seen it get passed yet. We'll see where the future leads. Geoff Johns is in charge now at Warner Brothers with DC Comics, and he worked with Donner way back in the day.[23] He's a real comic-book guy, so I'm really rooting for him. If he can just stick with his intuition and not let anybody sway what he believes in…if he goes with his instinct, Geoff Johns will be great and DC Comics and Superman will be fine.

GB: *After 40 years, what are your overall reflections on the making of* **Superman: The Movie?**
MM: The whole thing was such an adventure for me. Looking back, it definitely was a special time in my life. I'd never been to England before; it was my first time working with Englishmen. Geoffrey Unsworth was such a calm person. What a gentleman. He did his job calmly, and he was first-class. [Camera operator] Peter MacDonald too – all the boys were pros. Good memories. The whole experience was such a wonderful journey in my lifetime, for sure.

"I had no idea that [Reeve] would end up looping my voice. Of course it bothered me that he did that. They didn't even tell me that they were going to do it. So that was kind of a let-down."

JEFF EAST

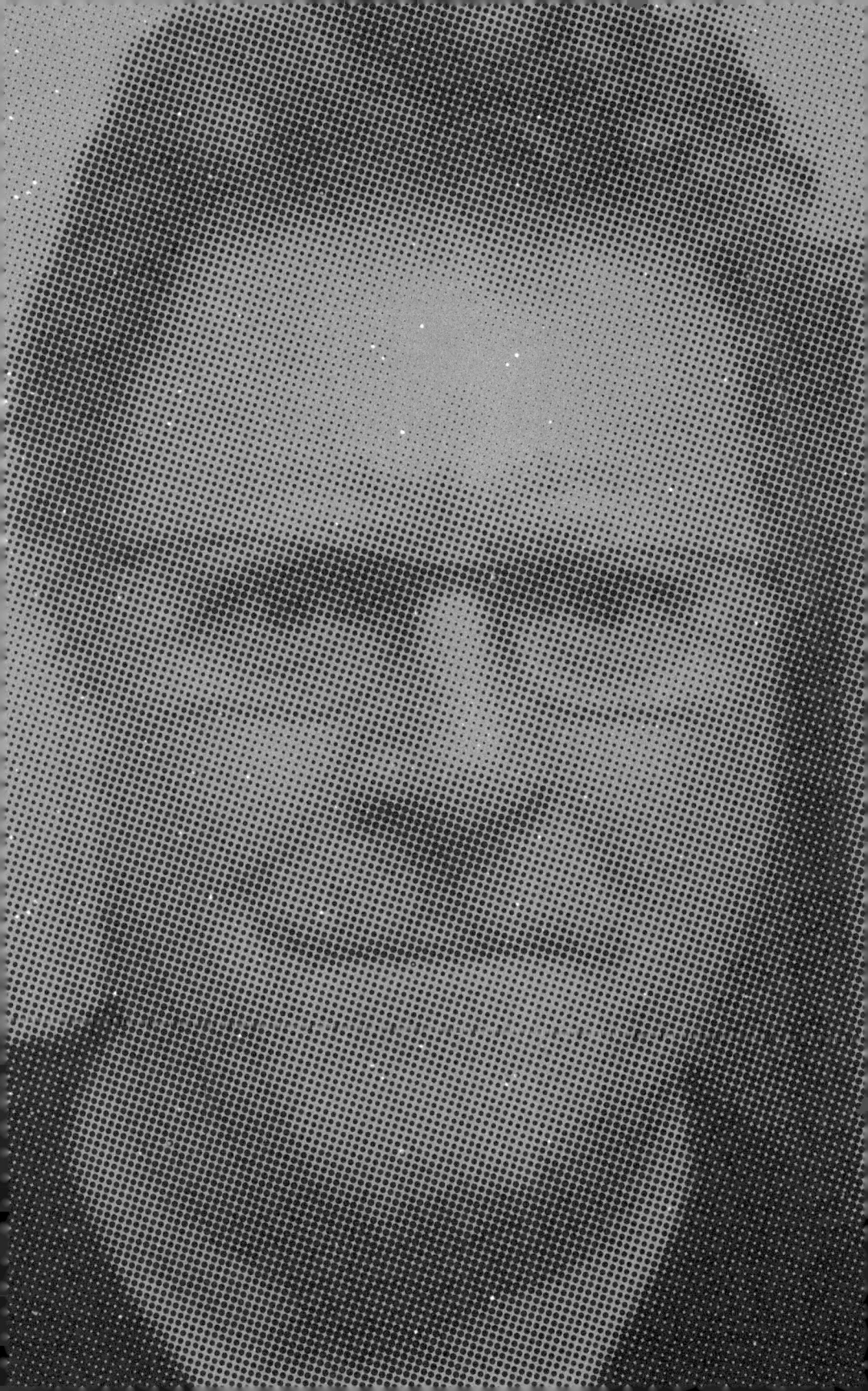

JEFF EAST
YOUNG CLARK KENT

Gary Bettinson: The casting director, Lynn Stalmaster, initially brought you in to audition for Jimmy Olsen rather than Young Clark Kent – is that correct?
Jeff East: That's right. I got a phone call from my agent saying that Lynn Stalmaster wants to have a meeting with me in regard to *Superman*. And so I went to the meeting, and Lynn says, 'I'd like for you to come back; the director wants to meet with you along with the producers.' So I said, 'Great.' I didn't know what role I was up for; I assumed it was Jimmy Olsen. I didn't know there was a young Clark Kent role. So I came back and I went to the audition and met with Dick Donner. They handed me some sides to the script. They didn't actually have me read; I just talked to them. Then the director took a photo of me, and then he put my photo next to Christopher Reeve's. And he says, 'You guys have similar features, I can see you being a young Christopher Reeve.' I said, 'Who's Christopher Reeve?' He says, 'He's our Superman.' I said, 'Oh wow, that's great. What role are you wanting *me* to do?' 'Well, we were thinking of you as the young Clark Kent.' I said, 'I don't have to wear an outfit or anything, do I? No crazy cape or anything like that?' He said, 'No, no, you don't have to wear a cape, you're the human Superman.' 'Oh, well then, fine.' He said, 'Have you got a passport?' I said, 'Yeah, as a matter of fact I do.' 'Great, because you're getting on an airplane tomorrow and you're flying to London.' I swear it was that quick.

GB: Were you plunged into shooting as soon as you arrived in London?
JE: I flew in to London, and I went in and had a hair test. I had blonde hair, so they tried to dye my hair but that didn't work. They put wigs on me. There was one test after another. And they were testing fake noses – they wanted to change my nose to make me look more like Chris. They had me meet with Chris, and get to know him. I thought, 'Oh, my.' And then, within a week of that, I started shooting the Fortress of Solitude scenes. I kept saying to Donner, 'How come you hired *me*? Why would you hire me to play this part?' He said, 'I saw you in a film called *The Hazing* and I really thought you brought your character to life; I want the same thing in *Superman*.' Anyway, we started shooting.

We were in London; I was probably there for a month shooting the interior of the Fortress of Solitude scenes. And those shots took forever. We would shoot one shot during the entire day. So, a role that probably would have taken a week to do ended up taking a year. It was nuts. I started in April of '77, and I was still shooting in October of '77. They flew me into London; then I flew back to L.A.; then they brought me back to London; then up to Canada for a month; and then back to London to shoot the creation of the Fortress of Solitude. I loved every minute of it, but I didn't think it was going to take *that* long. Usually when I worked on a film in those days it was seven to eight weeks; that was a normal shoot for me. *Superman* was like a lifetime. It was crazy.

GB: Were the wardrobe tests very extensive?
JE: It was trial-and-error. The whole film was trial-and-error. The nosepiece went wrong once in a while; they couldn't get it right. In some of the shots my nose is blue! We had problems with the wig – sometimes it looked too short, sometimes too long. I had to get up two or three hours before everyone else and go to the set for all the make-up and the hair. I did not enjoy that part of the process. Once I was in costume, I felt like I was Clark. It helped me get into the role better. But the process of it was a pain in the ass. And I remember the costume designers talked specifically about the shirt I wore. They wanted it to be loose-fitting because they had to put these cable wires underneath and lift me up to do the train sequence. They had to have a shirt that would cover up the wires. And the shirt had to be red; they wanted it red.

GB: Yes, your costuming – the red shirt and lumber jacket, the blue, red and yellow material in Young Clark Kent's bag – foreshadows the costume that Christopher Reeve wears later in the film.
JE: Right. That material in Clark's bag is supposed to be his Superman outfit. You know, when I was cast I told Donner: 'I don't want to wear a costume. No way. I'm not wearing a costume.' And he said, 'Don't worry about it; I won't make you wear the costume.' That was one thing I never wanted to do. I feel sorry for the girl [Melissa Benoist] who plays Supergirl in the television series.[24] She looks so uncomfortable in that outfit. She's cute as hell and she is a good actress, but you can just tell she probably dreads putting that thing on. I would not have liked that.

GB: Once you were cast, were you given Mario Puzo's draft of the screenplay?
JE: Yes, I was given the Mario Puzo script. Mankiewicz was working on the script at that time. See, I was cast before even Margot was cast. They'd given me the Mario Puzo script, and Margot was testing for the role of Lois Lane. And Margot and I flew to London on the same airplane together. We stayed at the same hotel the night that we got there, and so I got to know Margot right away. She was nervous as hell, because she was testing the next day. I was laughing, because I was already locked in. I told her, 'I'm hoping you

get the part, because you're great,' and she *was* great. Anyway, the Puzo script was different than the script they eventually shot. The Daily Planet scenes were not quite the same. The earlier part of the script was still the same. They didn't change much of that. It was all the stuff at the Daily Planet between Lois and Clark that was changed by Mankiewicz. And I had seen both versions of the script, because they kept giving me changes. So as I'm proceeding through the film, I'm seeing new script pages and new scenes. And actually the Lex Luthor stuff was all different. Puzo's script was pretty meandering. It was a pretty big script. But it was cool to be involved with something Puzo wrote.

GB: Were your scenes filmed as Puzo had written them?
JE: Almost verbatim. I don't think Mankie had anything to do with the Young Clark Kent scenes. He might have put in a few of the lines, like 'How did you get here so fast?' 'I ran.' He might have done that. But his main changes were to the romance between Lois and Clark.

GB: Once you were cast in **Superman***, how did you prepare for the role?*
JE: My main thing was to try to capture Chris's spirit. So I spent a lot of time with Chris. There were hours where we just hung out and got to know each other. When I got to Canada, Donner wanted me to read some comic books, because he wanted to bring some of this comic-book feeling to it. It didn't really affect me. I truly mainly worked on the actual character of Clark and how he would feel if he was in the situations depicted in the script. I would not have gotten that from any comic book. My preparation mainly involved discussions with Dick Donner, and just kind of working on it myself. Donner helped me a lot. He said, 'Really, just play yourself, Jeff, and it will naturally happen.' And Glenn Ford was great. When he got there, it was so easy. All the scenes I did with Glenn Ford I think were shot in one take. He was such a pro. The same with Phyllis Thaxter.

GB: You were 20 years old at the time?
JE: Yes. 20.

GB: You'd already had quite a lot of acting experience by then. But do you remember learning anything specific about acting from watching Glenn Ford work?
JE: I learned from Ford that even when the camera is off, you can still be in character. He had a lot of that going for him. He just had this demeanour. You know, small talk with him while we were working just didn't really happen. He wanted to keep it within the energy of the scene. I understood that. A lot of actors work that way. I wasn't used to that, so I kind of had to get used to it. It wasn't that he was cold; he was just trying to stay in character. So I went with it. And Donner really didn't have to direct us in that scene. He knew that there was chemistry between the two of us. It was brilliant casting, I think.

GB: You say that Donner told you to basically be yourself. Was that the primary piece of direction he gave you?
JE: Well, he said, 'Think of it a little bit like what you went through as a young actor. When you were acting, playing Huckleberry Finn,[25] think about when all your friends in school made fun of you about your movie career. You kind of went through that in real life.' I said, 'Yeah, that's true.' He kind of got personal with me. Dick and I were good friends. He knew stuff that I'd been through; he knew I'd been acting since I was 14, and he said, 'Clark's situation is sort of like that. I want that feeling. It's like you're frustrated, Jeff.' It wasn't that hard for me to understand. And it was well written, it was well directed and you had great actors like Ford and Thaxter. How can you go wrong? Donner kept encouraging me. We would get up at five in the morning and do shots of the wheat fields, to catch the sun.

GB: Those shots are astonishing.
JE: Oh yeah. We shot the Smallville scenes in Lethbridge, Alberta. And Geoff Unsworth was great. Geoff had a funny, dry sense of humour and he was always very professional. Peter MacDonald, the camera operator, was great. We had to do some crazy stuff. The scene when Clark races the train was a very tricky stunt. We spent two weeks just practicing that stunt before we shot it. It was tough trying to get me to hold still and not swing from the wires. That was one of the hard things they couldn't figure out how to do. And I had to touch the ground a little bit with my feet just so that it would work. They were dragging me at 35 miles per hour. And they were trying to figure out how to do the moment when Clark jumps in front of the train. We did it backwards and then we did it forwards, and then the train would go backwards and then the train would go forwards. It was crazy. It was not like they do it today. It was an old-fashioned way of making movies.

GB: And the shot of Clark kicking the football into orbit?
JE: That was easy. That was done with a canon buried in the ground. There was a cylinder that comes out and it looks like a football. And then they actually had me go out there and stand right by the hole where the canon is and pretend like I'm kicking the ball. I did a simulation kick without the ball in my hands, and that's when you see the ball come right out of the ground and the canon shoots it off. That sucker went all the way. They didn't keep it in the movie, but I swear to God, the ball actually knocked the Smallville sign off the grain elevator a quarter of a mile away. That was funny. And then of course I had a little thing with Diane Sherry who played Lana Lang. It just happened; we were young and going to breakfast with each other and then going to dinner with each other. One thing led to another. She decided to tell her boyfriend about it, and he gets all mad and comes up to the set! So the producers had to hide me out for a couple of days in the hotel. They didn't want any black eyes or anything like that while we were shooting.

GB: As you say, the Smallville scenes were shot on location. Was there a marked difference between shooting on location and shooting on the 007 stage at Pinewood?

JE: On the stage it was a much longer process. Shooting in the studio is more business-like: you go to work at a certain time and you leave at a certain time. The crew doesn't hang out with you at night; they go home. But when we were on location in Canada, it felt more like a normal movie-making experience to me. In Canada, everybody got real close; everybody stayed in the same hotel and got to know each other. There was a kind of camaraderie that came from being on location. So yeah, the feeling is definitely different. Now, the crew in London, they were all the Pinewood guys. They were very different from the American stage guys that I had worked with. Before *Superman* I had done a lot of films with Disney, and working on the stages there with their technical people was very different. I think the English crew members were technically better than the American technicians when it came to special effects. The English crews seemed to know something a little bit more than the Americans. I think that's why *Star Wars* and *Superman* did so well, because those guys knew what they were doing.[26] I'm not sure they could have technically pulled that off in America at that time. The Superman producers brought those British guys over to Canada too, and it shows in the movie. Those guys were the best in the game at that time. You couldn't get any better.

GB: You share an important scene with Brando. Were your shots filmed separately or did you shoot the scene together?

JE: Brando is the only cast member I never met. In fact, years later I used to go to Jack Nicholson's house on Mulholland Drive, and I knew that Brando lived right next door to Jack. But I never went over to introduce myself. I did a film for Jack [*Blue Champagne*], so I knew Jack real well. He'd say, 'Your father lives right next door!' I'd say, 'I don't even know him!'

GB: Richard Lester was enlisted as a producer on **Superman: The Movie.** *He directed some of your scenes, didn't he?*

JE. Yes. I was not involved when the big fight happened between Donner and Salkind, thank God. But I had to go back to shoot some of the special-effects shots for the train sequence and the Fortress of Solitude, and the producers had Lester direct those shots. Donner directed the shots where I throw the crystal that builds the Fortress of Solitude; I remember him sitting there coaching me through it. As I remember, it was just one day that Lester was on the set directing instead of Donner, and it felt weird. It felt like second unit. But I was not privy to all the brouhaha that was going on at that time.

GB: You mentioned spending a lot of time with Christopher Reeve. Can you specify what that preparatory work involved?

JE: He was real interested in how I was going to portray him. He was very concerned about that. He wanted to play that role [Young Clark Kent] himself. He told the producers he wanted to play both roles, but they wouldn't let him do it. He was very concerned about my mannerisms, even the way I walked – the gait in my walk was a concern to him. We talked about it. And I would watch him. We'd play chess with each other, and he was very good at chess. Chris was really smart, a very intelligent guy and very well educated. I was a little different: I'm more Midwestern, he was very East Coast. I just had to get used to his style, his way of speaking. And boy, I had no idea that they would, at the end there, end up looping my voice.[27] Actually, I kind of understand it, because from the time you go from me to him in the movie, it's almost immediate. My voice *is* different than his. And the looping of my voice was something that *he* wanted to do, and the producers went ahead and did it. And it worked – he did it well. But of course it bothered me that he did that. They didn't even tell me that they were going to do it. And I'm not sure when that decision was made. You know, I think it would have been neat if they had called me and said, 'Hey, this is what we're going to do, and this is why we're going to do it.' But they didn't. So that was kind of a let-down. They kind of let me down. I didn't hear about it until the actual premiere of the film. It was in Washington, DC, and Marc McClure called me and said, 'Jeff, you're not going to believe this. Chris looped your voice.' I was like, 'Oh God.' Yeah, that was pretty amazing. But the thing is, it happened, you know?

GB: Was it the producers' responsibility to inform you that your performance would be post-dubbed?
JE: You would think. The producer or the director. I don't think it was a malicious act. It was just that Chris felt, and the studio felt, that the voice needed to be the same as Chris's. Chris has got a higher pitch and mine is lower. So, there you go. I'm not sure that it took away from the performance. I don't think it really matters. The scenes are what they are. It plays out fine. Ninety per cent of acting is really what you do with your face and your body, not what you're saying. Film acting is more of an expressive art. But, you know, it did happen, and of course I wasn't real happy about it with Chris. But over the years I got over it, and we saw each other now and then. Of course, I got involved with helping him raise money for his foundation. So I moved on.

GB: You were in contact with him after his accident?
JE: Oh yeah. I went up to Toronto to raise quite a bit of money for his foundation, and we met each other in L.A.[28] I definitely wanted to help. That was very important to be involved with that.

GB: I understand that Robin Williams helped to dissolve the tension between you and Christopher Reeve?
JE: Yes, actually at the premiere of the film in L.A., Robin was at the party. He could

tell there was some tension between us. I was mad. I was pissed off. And Chris was like, 'Well, we probably should have told you, blah blah blah,' and I said, 'Yeah, they should have told me!' Because, you know, the Smallville scenes are a large chunk of the film, and it was an important role. Anyway, Robin says, 'I was Chris's roommate in college,' and he got me laughing about what happened. He broke the ice between us. I liked Robin a lot, he was a good guy.

GB: Apparently, Hackman, Brando and Kidder kept the mood light during shooting, whereas Reeve was less mirthful.
JE: That's right. It's very true. I got to know everybody working on the film, even though I'm not in any scenes with Hackman or Chris or Ned Beatty. But we were all on the set together; we all shot at the same time. So we all got to know each other pretty well over that year-long period. Gene cracked me up. Gene would pull practical jokes on people. He was always trying to keep people laughing, Margot was always trying to do it too and Chris would get mad at them. Chris and Gene got at it one day; they came to blows. But that wore off. Then Gene and Ned Beatty and Valerie Perrine came with us to Canada. Man, they were just partying, having a good time. Larry Hagman and Valerie got drunk in my Winnebago one day.[29] We're supposed to be working and they're partying in the Winnebago. It was pretty fun. Valerie was a real funny gal.

GB: Did you have a sense during production that **Superman** *would be successful?*
JE: You knew when you were working on it that it was an important film. You knew just by the budget and by the huge crew that you were working with, and the amount of time they took with it, and all the actors that were in it. I figured, yeah, this is going to be a pretty big film. It turned out better than I thought, though, to be honest with you. I was really pleasantly surprised when I saw the film. I thought, 'Wow, that really worked' – beyond what we thought when we were working on it. Even with Chris dubbing my voice, I was okay with it. *Before* I saw the movie, I was more upset. But when I saw it, I was okay with it. It still worked. Because I knew it was me; it was still me. And it's amazing how many times – if I go to a bar or a club or a party or to someone's house – I get introduced as Superman. I'm like, 'No, don't introduce me like that, okay?' But it happens, and I guess it's a compliment. I've done 40 films, but that's the only one they bring up. It will live with me for the rest of my life. I was just glad the film turned out so well. I'm happy to be a part of it.

> "There was a lot of gossip flying around on the set. I know about men standing on the side of the set [looking] suspiciously like they had come out of a gangster movie. They looked like they were packing guns."

— SARAH DOUGLAS

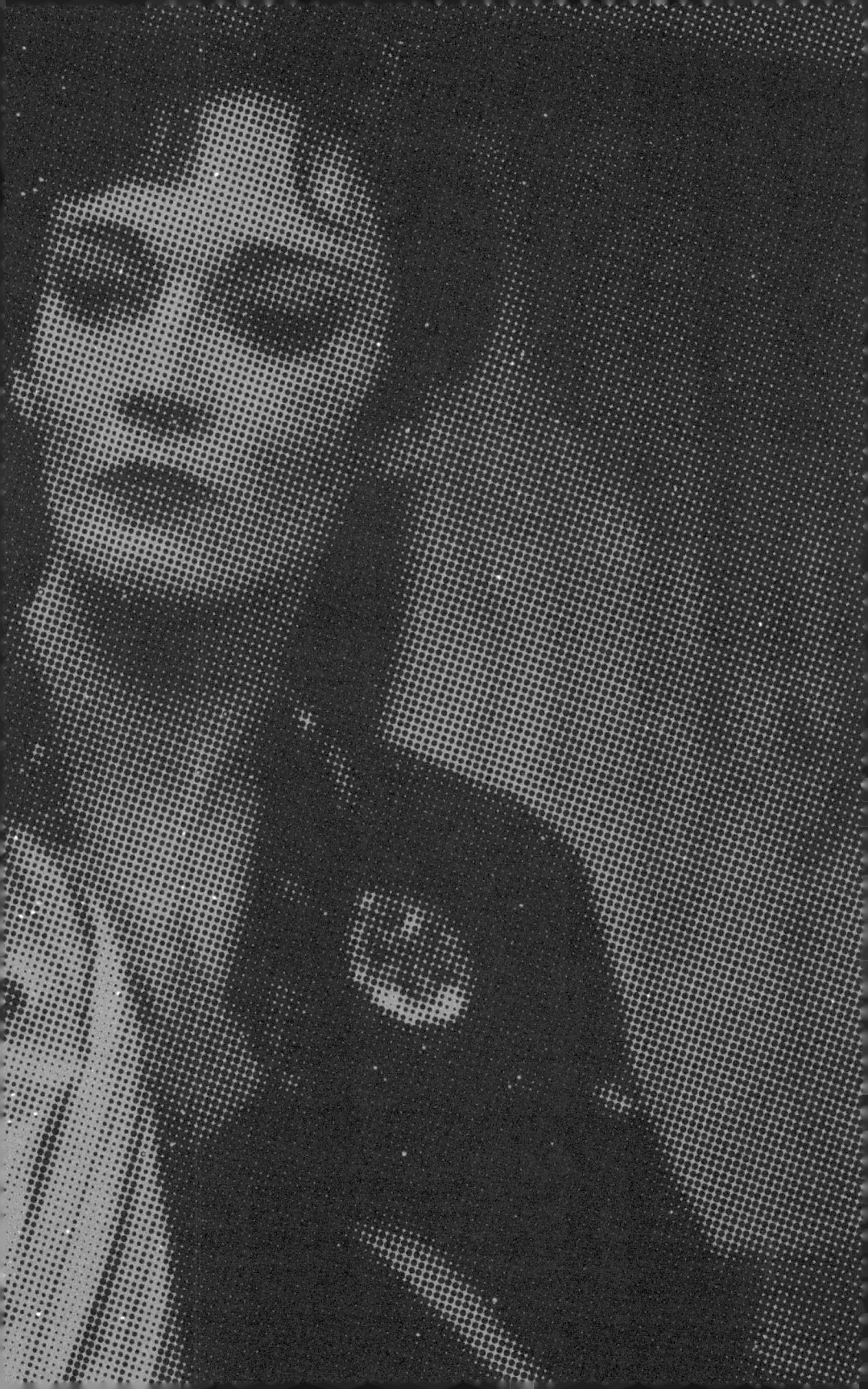

SARAH DOUGLAS
URSA

Gary Bettinson: I understand that you didn't have a formal screen test for **Superman.**
Sarah Douglas: No, I didn't. I was right in the midst of filming *The People That Time Forgot* in the Canaries, which was why I didn't have any kind of formal screen test for *Superman*. Then I came back to England. I was shooting *The People That Time Forgot* at Pinewood Studios; the Superman producers were auditioning people at Shepperton studios. I was shooting every day and so I wasn't available to audition, and the Superman producers weren't about to spend money doing a screen test in the evening, basically. They kept scheduling me for a meeting and cancelling. So when I finally got to meet Donner and the producers, I was in such a pissy mood. Unfortunately I do have a streak in me which can be slightly withering, I've been told – if I care to put somebody in their place I don't have to do much but give a look. And it seems that that's how it was when I arrived for the meeting with Donner. I just thought, 'Who is this bloody man?' He comes over from California, he's wearing these blue-tinted glasses, which I thought were totally pretentious on a dark afternoon, and he has this slightly too-long silvery hair. My whole attitude towards him was one of slight contempt. I certainly didn't suffer fools gladly then, and I think that was part of what got me the role. Anyway, I did a little read for Donner and the producers, and I did some flying tests. Those were the only two things that I did. And I started shooting *Superman* the day after I finished *The People That Time Forgot*.

GB: At what stage were you cast in **Superman***? Were Terence Stamp and Jack O'Halloran already on board?*
SD: No. I know that Margot wasn't cast. I know they hadn't found their Lois Lane.

GB: Was there a possibility that you might audition for Lois Lane?
SD: Oh, no. Let's put it like this: I was always the good girl who was a bit naughty on the side – that was the kind of character I often portrayed then. I was about 27 years old. I'd already been working for a good few years, and I really did play the kind of English Rose

who always had a little bit of a naughty spark. And then after I did *Superman*, I played the evil wicked queen forever more.

GB: *Was there an alternative look for the Kryptonian villains than the one seen in the films?*
SD: No, there were no alternatives. I had very long hair from *The People That Time Forgot* but nobody ever said 'Get your hair cut', and so I didn't. Every day on *Superman* I would go through agony as they used a million hair grips and pin curls to put my hair into a tight short-cropped wig. It was so uncomfortable. Also, they had designed that fabulous costume, but they seemed not to take into consideration the harness that we had to wear for the flying scenes. I couldn't wear a full harness, which goes from the chest down to the hips, because I had those slits up the sides of my costume. The harness would have been visible. So they gave me a tiny little girdle instead, a little suspender belt, which I could just about wear. Getting into make-up and costume was a long drawn-out process, but the minute that costume went on, there was that magical thing that happens to some of us, where it was no longer me. I look at Ursa now and it's not me. The costume changes you. If Ursa looks mean and evil, it had to do with the fact that I had been in make-up since 5.30am, I had got a very uncomfortable wig on, my face was coated in white powder, my eyebrows were stuck up, my false nails had been baked onto my fingers, I was wearing a tight harness and I wanted to go to the loo and couldn't. One didn't have to reach too deep to find the emotion! With the costumes and flying, they really hadn't figured it out when we started filming. On the very first day of filming, when Superman raises his arms to fly, Chris Reeve was perspiring. Well, Superman doesn't sweat. So they had to stop everything, and work out how they could ensure that he never had any kind of perspiration marks on his costume.

GB: *What version of the screenplay were you first presented with? Did you build your portrayal primarily from the screenplay?*
SD: I remember we were presented with two scripts in cheap leather-bound folders with 'Superman I' and 'Superman II' on the front. I can remember being very impressed with that, because I'd never had two scripts for a job before. I became very close to [screenwriters] Leslie and David Newman, and I know that Leslie Newman was the one who really came up with who my character was. I mean, Ursa was a little bit of Leslie's fantasy. The Newmans were very much the ones who created the way Ursa looked and behaved. And then Terence Stamp is the one who really set the tone for me. Rather like Ursa and Non, I sort of followed in his wake. I remember Terry talking to Jack and I and saying that we are aliens, and there has to be a difference between us and the regular folk. He was the one that said we should have a fluidity of movement and walk together in unison. It's a very tiny little detail, but it's something that I consciously worked on. When you see the three of us moving, we do sort of move in unison as a team, which

was Terry's idea. But the minute they said 'Cut,' he went back to telling me wicked stories about Julie Christie and things like that. Of course, being next to him was a daily delight, because I had grown up worshipping him. I was transported back to the days of *Blue* and *Far from the Madding Crowd*, when I would fantasize over Terence Stamp. And suddenly here was this man who had just come back from India; he'd been gone for seven years living in some ashram.[30] He had come back from India, and he was full of mint tea and chanting and the like, and he wore a bit of orange here and there. He still had handmade shoes. I remember thinking, 'God, he might have given it all up but he's still got handmade shoes!' But he was absolutely a delight. There was a calmness about him and also a wickedness about him, which was lovely.

GB: What did you decide was the nature of Ursa's relationship to Zod and Non? To your mind, was she romantically attracted to Zod?
SD: I decided that I admired Zod enormously. I had very, very little time for Non. He was just a stupid oaf, in my mind. But there was definitely an admiration for Zod. I don't think I ever considered that Ursa was romantically involved with him, because I would have liked to have thought that her ultimate goal would be for her to be victorious.

GB: You mean she might usurp him at some point?
SD: Exactly.

GB: I imagine that you have vivid memories of working with Brando.
SD: Oh, I was so overwhelmed by Brando, because to me – to my generation – he was this enormous superstar. He had an aura about him, and I just soaked him up. Gene Hackman I became very friendly with, and that was more like hanging out with your genial uncle. I really enjoyed him. But Brando was – my goodness, you know? He really came at it – and I can't speak for him, obviously – but it appeared like he just thought, 'What a bloody ridiculous thing, this whole thing.' The fact that they had painted and carpeted his corridor at Shepperton, from his dressing room to the set, while the rest of the studio looked like hell. And of course he didn't learn his lines. He travelled with a girl who wrote the big cards with his dialogue written on. I remember him telling me, 'If you look at *The Missouri Breaks*, you can see my lines written on the back of the fence near Jack Nicholson.' And he said, 'If you think that's bad, in *Last Tango in Paris* I had all the words written down the side of Maria Schneider's body, and I'm reading them as I'm kissing her.' He was a very witty man. I've lived in Hollywood for twenty years and I've met many movie stars, but Brando had a magnetism about him that I've never really met again. I describe Gene Hackman as being 'regular folk', but Brando had some extra little something, an aura, and he brought it to the set. He was very generous and very aware. He was an absolute delight, just fabulous. I was also excited that Trevor Howard was going to work on *Superman*, because he and Brando had both been in *Mutiny on the*

Bounty. I was excited by that, because they hadn't seen each other since then. When we shot the opening sequence of *Superman*, all the actors were there with Brando. And I seem to recall that Trevor Howard and Brando didn't seem to be that comfortable with each other. Why that would be, I don't know.

GB: They clashed, reportedly, on Mutiny on the Bounty.
SD: Oh, did they? So maybe it was that.

GB: Did working with Hackman give you new insights about acting?
SD: He was very, very well prepared. I've worked with actors that have these great 'methods' and it's rather intense on the set, but there was none of that with Hackman. Hackman was another of my great heroes. I'm afraid that in between takes, we were all hysterical all of the time, laughing and enjoying ourselves. We all had a good time together. I don't know what I learned from Hackman other than to be prepared. You can get away with having a bit of a laugh or gossiping in between takes, as long as you're prepared for the moment the cameras start rolling. The preparation is the important thing. Now, Christopher, on the other hand, was very straight. The rest of us were just ridiculous; we all carried on. Christopher was a rather gawky young American. But of course, Christopher's great friend was Robin Williams, and if he was friends with Robin Williams then there must have been another side to him that we didn't see.

GB: I gather that you were on set for Christopher Reeve's very first day of shooting. Was this the first time you met him?
SD: Yes, I was there for his first day. I would have met him a week or two earlier for the costume fitting. And periodically, because he was going through screen tests with different Lois Lanes, I would bump into him. We were all – not naïve and young – but we were all in this big adventure together, so it was like the first day at school. Everybody was a little bit shy at the beginning, and a bit nervous. My first meeting with Chris wasn't anything spectacular; it was just 'Hey', and there was Chris. I remember meeting Margot, because I remember her bow legs. I was fascinated with the fact that she had come from Calgary and she sort of walked like a cowgirl. And indeed she continued to do that, even when dressed as Lois Lane, which I thought was fabulous. She looked just a little bit klutzy. We were all just a little tight band, which was lovely. We all started on the first day of shooting and we all ended on the last day, on *Superman II*. We were in it together.

GB: How much interaction did you have with the Salkinds and Spengler?
SD: Well, I didn't have the interaction that the others had. I was slightly intimidated by them because they were 'the producers.' The other cast members had very bad feelings towards them, especially when we lost Donner and he was replaced by Lester. I was

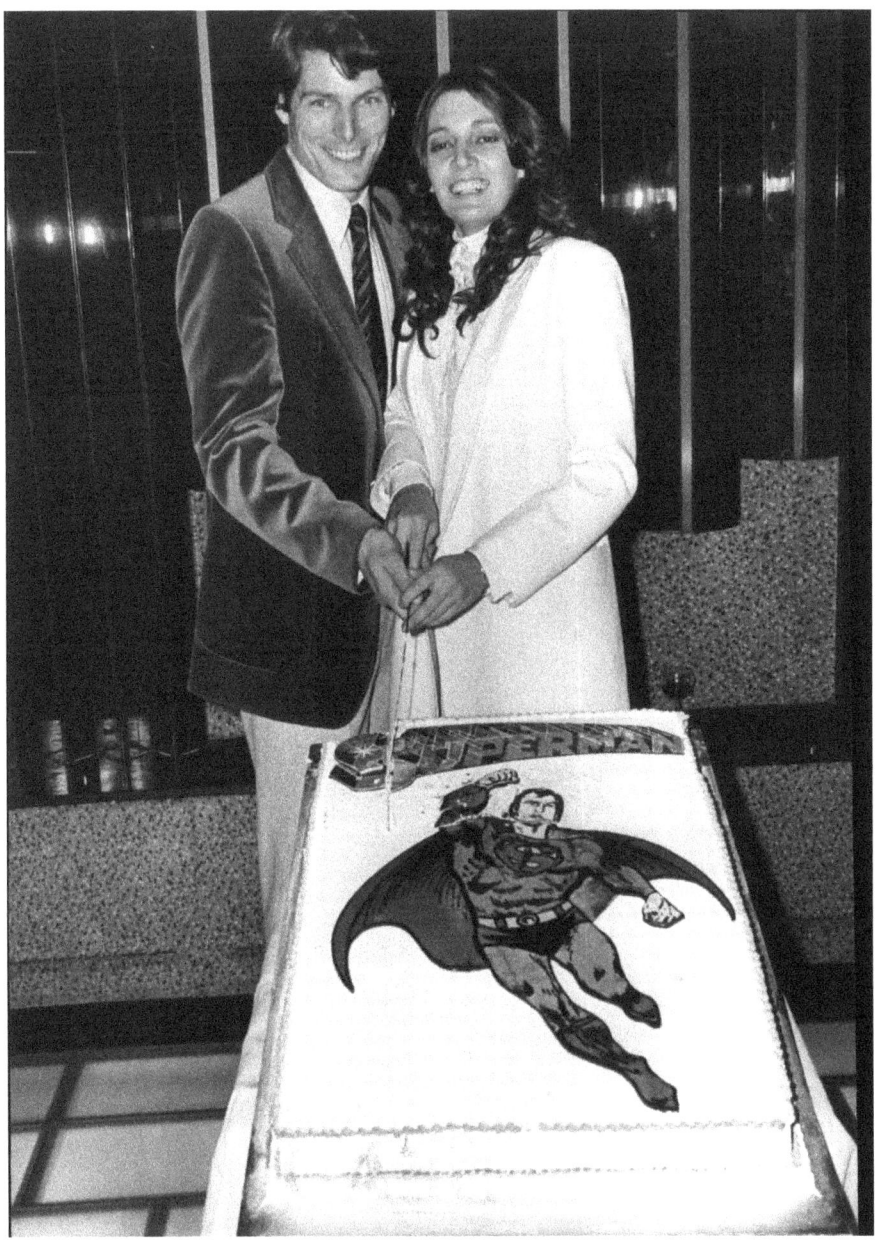

Figure 25: Christopher Reeve and Sarah Douglas celebrate the opening of *Superman*. Photo: Phillip Jackson/ANL/REX/Shutterstock

not part of that kind of thing, because I didn't have the same bond with Donner that they all had. I loved him, and I loved working with him, but I didn't spend the evenings with him like the others did. I never saw any of them in the evening. They were all on location; they all had per diem, they all lived in nice places, and they all hung out together because they were away from home and didn't know anybody else. They had a camaraderie. I was the only one that wasn't on-location, and after the day's shooting I went home and made supper. But anyway – the Salkinds were the Salkinds. I had heard all the stories about them. Jack [O'Halloran] got into lots of lovely arguments with the Salkinds. I don't know which one it was that he picked up by the collar and threatened because his money hadn't arrived. And there was a lot of gossip flying around on the set. I know about men turning up in the middle of the night shoot who looked suspiciously like they had just come out of a gangster movie; they were standing on the side of the set and they all looked like they were packing guns. I'm sure they weren't, but there was a lot of talk about what was going on and who these people were. I never found out.

GB: Before **Superman: The Movie** *was released, Marlon Brando predicted that the film would be successful; Margot Kidder apparently thought she was making a flop. When you were making the film, did you feel that it would be a success?*
SD: No. It wasn't until the very first cast screening at Tottenham Court Road that we saw that Superman could fly. It was absolutely not until then that we realized the film would work. I went to the cast and crew screening of *Star Wars*, because my husband at the time was in the first *Star Wars*, and I remember that opening sequence where the spaceship comes over your head and you duck, and you say, 'Whoa!' It was the same with Superman flying: you just thought, 'Wow.' So no, I had no sense as we were making the film that it would be such a success.

GB: Was Richard Lester temperamentally very different from Donner?
SD: Yes. You have to remember, we were imagining that we were going to get this guy from *A Hard Day's Night* – a sort of laid-back, funny, amusing person, and he was very much the opposite of that. He seemed quite uptight. If I was to draw the two of them, I'd draw Donner with long hair and the T-shirt and the tinted glasses, and Lester would have the suit and the tie tightly done up. That's how I saw them.

GB: I've been told that Lester didn't like much rehearsal.
SD: No. But there wasn't really much to rehearse. You're only talking about a page or half a page. There were no great big sequences. The great big sequences with stunts were, of course, all rehearsed; but that was all about the stunts, and your stunt double is getting in there and rehearsing for you. The stunt doubles do the dodgy stuff, and then you just come in at the last moment. I do remember on the backlot of Chobham Common when I was about to blow a helicopter out of the sky. I was just standing there with Stamp and

we'd set up the whole scene, and then suddenly they called for Stamp's stunt double. I thought, 'Why is there a stunt double for him?' And the next minute they called 'Action' and I found out why! There were all these explosions going on under our feet and around us, and there were bits of peat and crap flying around, and it got into my eyes and under my wig and into my costume. It's the one sequence where you can see my eyes fluttering. I was very naïve in those days and I was willing to try everything. And it's not easy to say 'No, this is dangerous, I won't do it,' because you've got a great big crew and directors and producers saying, 'Come on, get on with it' – and you're rather apt to go for the shots that possibly are a little bit less than safe. And certainly on *Superman* we had a few of those.

One of the great moments making *Superman II* happened on the set where they built Metropolis. For the scene when the three of us villains are blowing everybody away in the street, they built a New York street on the backlot with all the shops in. One of the shops was Mothercare. It was the first time, I think I'm right in saying, that they had done a product placement; there was quite a bit of product placement in *Superman*. And the shops were filled with wonderful products. But nobody bothered to put a back on the shops, and when we came on the set the following morning everything had been stolen! The silly buggers.

GB: *You were the only member of the cast to participate in the international promotional tour for* Superman II. *Why was that?*
SD: The producers were not going to risk sending Christopher or Margot around the world, because both of them were absolutely on the Donner trail then, and quite rightly waving a flag and talking about him. Back then, nobody knew about the behind-the-scene problems. The public just assumed that Richard Lester had directed *Superman II* – the word was not out in any way that Richard Donner had had anything to do with it. I merrily went marching around the world one-and-a-half times over a period of nine months selling *Superman II* for the producers. The publicity tour started in Australia, and then we opened the film in a different country just about every other week.

GB: *Did Lester accompany you on the tour?*
SD: I did it almost all single-handedly. Lester turned up in one country; I think it might have been Japan. He was a man of few words, and I barely saw him. But in Australia, New Zealand, South Africa, Japan and all those places, I was completely on my own. In Japan, I remember, the censors cut out the sequence on the surface of the moon where I kick the astronaut. It was considered too violent, and the idea of a woman acting violently against a man was a problem. So that scene was cut out.

GB: The film opened around the world before it was released in the United States. Was this strategy designed to build anticipation for the US release?
SD: I believe so. The producers were trying to do something different, but it didn't work. Well, I mean, it obviously worked because everybody went to see *Superman II*. But American audiences were the last to see it, and they weren't best pleased. There was no fanfare at the opening in America, because everybody in America had kind of seen the film or heard all about it. The opening in America was very much a damp squib. I don't think we even had an opening in Los Angeles. The producers never tried that kind of release again.

GB: There is a deleted scene from **Superman II** *in which the Kryptonian villains survive at the climax.*
SD: Yes, there was a very strong possibility that the villains were going to come back in *Superman III*. The writers were setting it up at the end of *Superman II* for the three villains to come back. But then the ending was reshot so that Ursa just disappeared over the edge. By *Superman III*, Christopher had pretty much approval of everything – script, cast, everything. And I know that he wasn't overly thrilled that the super villains almost overshadowed Superman in *Superman II*. That's why the first poster that came out – which was a shot, between Superman's legs, of the three villains – was cancelled. They withdrew that poster and released one that was more focused on Superman. Now, this is just my interpretation. However, I do remember reshooting the ending of *Superman II*. You know, when I went to see *Superman II: The Donner Cut*, I just was delighted and thrilled.

GB: Do you have a preference for either version of **Superman II**?
SD: Oh yeah, I definitely have a preference for the Donner cut. Absolutely. Oh yes, because it was very much his vision. There is a certain magic to it, and also the fact that it's a little bit cobbled together here and there. I just think it's amazing to think that all that footage sat in a vault for all those years. None of us knew about it. There were rumours going around, but nobody knew that Donner had shot that much footage. I certainly hadn't realized that he had enough for practically a whole movie. For an actress – for any of us – to work on something as big as that with two completely different directors is an extraordinary, wonderful experience. And the audience's reactions are great. I must say I really and truly have not met anybody that hasn't said that they really like the Donner version.

GB: You've spoken to many people about **Superman** *over the years. Is it your impression that Ursa has been embraced by the public as a feminist hero?*
SD: Yes, absolutely. I was oblivious at the time to the impact that she made. I finished the movie and I went back to my little housewifery existence. I had no idea that Ursa

had such an impact, particularly on young men. What has really fascinated me more is the gay community. I've had endless, endless gay men telling me how important Ursa was to them, and how, when they were struggling with their sexuality, they looked to Ursa. It's something I haven't quite worked out. Certainly I had an impact but what is the impact? I don't know. The first time that I really started to notice it was when they said, 'You're a gay icon.' So I feel incredibly fortunate that I have this vast following of men. I mean, there are lots and lots of young women, too, that look to Ursa. As far as the feminist goes, Ursa is a role model for the strong woman not taking any crap. I'm absolutely delighted that somebody that is basically bad and evil and wicked has got such a following. It does seem that some part of Ursa's wickedness is obviously resonating with many, many women – and a lot of boys too! Her appeal is across the board, really, which is great.

GB: *Forty years on, how do you assess the impact that* **Superman** *has had on your life and career?*
SD: *Superman* really has always been there throughout my career. It's always been something that I used to get a little ticked off about, because I thought 'For God's sake, Ursa doesn't look like me, she's not me, why are people making this fuss?' Now I'm amazed by it and quite grateful for it. I wasn't very appreciative for many years, but now I think, 'How cool is that, to be connected with a film that just about everybody in the world has seen?' I'll tell you: I had a tough time in Hollywood a few years back. You don't have tough times in Hollywood; nobody talks about it. And I had befriended a very old lady who didn't know I was an actress, and she asked me if I could take her to the post office. I was extremely hard-up and I was going to sell my car – I had got it on the market that week. And she said, 'I hear you've got a car, a big old car, and perhaps you could take me to the post office. I've got a hundred books' – her husband had just died, and he was a poet – 'I've got a hundred books and I need to get them stamped and sent off to universities.' So I drove her and these books to the post office. And outside the post office was an old black tramp sitting on the ground. He was a bag of rags. And he stuck his hand up to me and said, 'Spare a quarter for a brother?' He didn't look up. I remember thinking, 'I've got five bucks in my pocket – what the hell, it can't get much worse. On the way back I shall give him some money.' And I took my old girl inside the post office, went back to the car, got the box full of books, came back, and as I handed the money down to the tramp, he looked up at me and said, 'You're Sarah Douglas. I love your work. I loved you in *Superman*.' And I was so overwhelmed. I couldn't believe it. He said, 'Can I help you?' and I said 'Sure.' He got up and came inside, and he was filthy. My old girl, Kate, was there, and I said to her, 'This is a new friend.' And there we stood: this old lady in her eighties, myself, and this old tramp, all of us sticking on stamps. At the end, Kate offered him ten bucks, and he said 'Oh no, no, no – it was just a pleasure to have met you in person, Ms. Douglas.' And off he went. Kate and I got in the car, and she

said to me: 'My dear, I don't know what you've done, but you've put a spring in his gait and a smile on his face. What a gift.' And it stuck with me forever more. Whether it be *Superman* or something else, the fact that you can touch somebody that you don't even know. It was a turning point for me at a very, very dark time. And *Superman* has allowed me that. I'm very lucky.

"*Forty years later it's still as popular as it was the day we did it. I can look at Superman today and say, "Show me a picture better than this" – technology-wise and acting-wise. You're never going to get another Christopher.*"

JACK O'HALLORAN

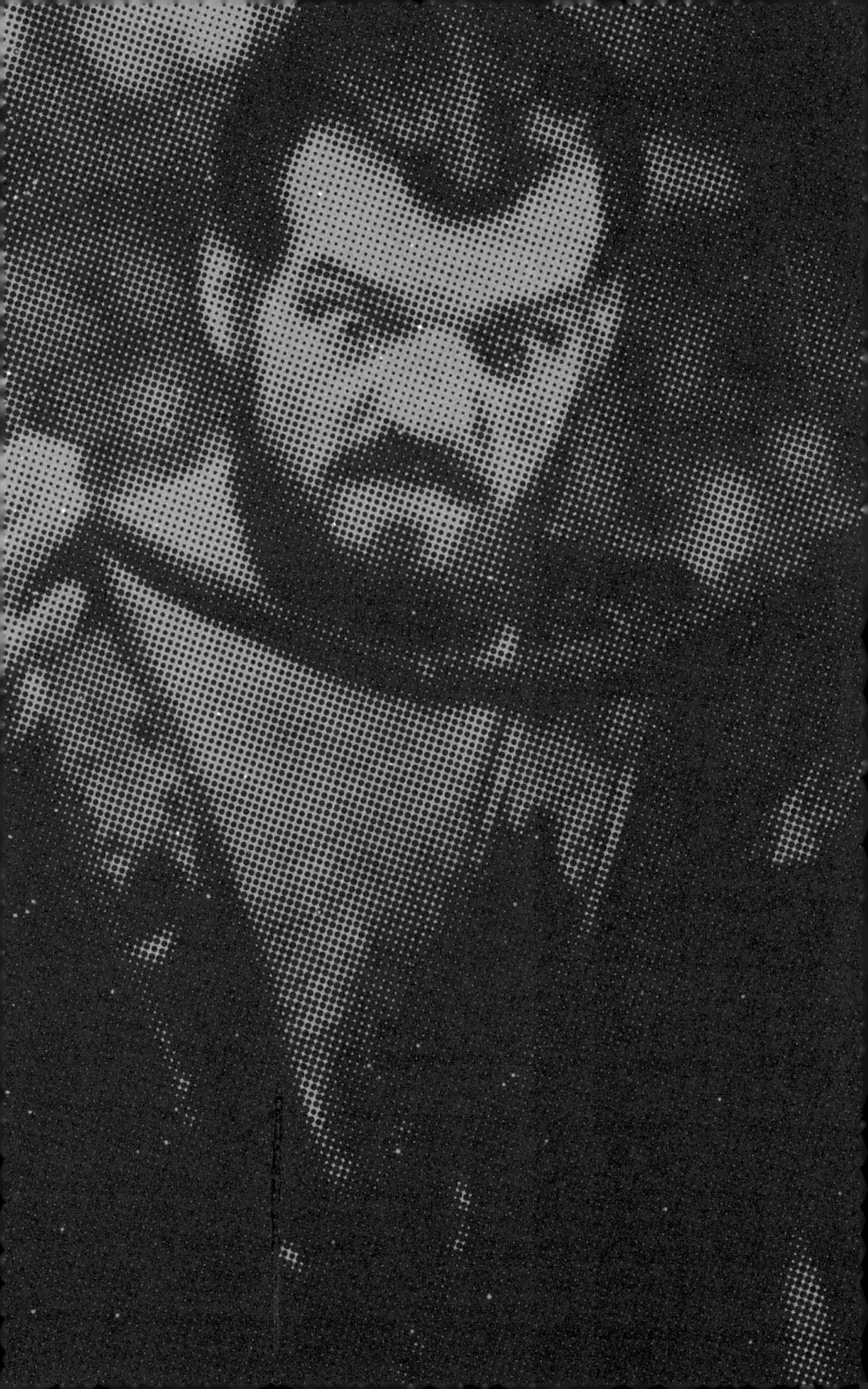

JACK O'HALLORAN
NON

Gary Bettinson: I gather that you were shooting March or Die *with Gene Hackman when you were first approached to appear in* Superman.
Jack O'Halloran: That's correct.

GB: Had Hackman recommended you to Richard Donner?
JO: No. I had a reputation as an actor already, because of *Farewell, My Lovely* and *King Kong*. When they were looking to cast the Superman film, they were looking for a villain that had some ability as an actor. And I liked the idea of Non. I liked the idea of him not talking. Among the three villains you had Zod, who was this maniacal individual, and you had Ursa who was a man-eater. There had to be one of us that children could relate to – I mean, we're talking about a picture that was going to reach a children's audience. I realized that Non could do things as a child does them. It would be like Lenny in *Of Mice and Men* – this menacing, brutish individual who has childlike mannerisms. In the original comic books, Non was a top scientist who had been lobotomized. Lobotomies can go a lot of ways: there are all kinds of varieties of them. I wanted to take Non's rational thinking process and bring it down to child level. He learns how to work his eyes like a child learns how to walk. In the scene alongside the truck [in *Superman II*], when he burns the first hole into the wood with his eyes, he acts like a child – he's like, 'Oh my God, I just did my first somersault.'[31]

GB: Does Non view Zod and Ursa as parental figures?
JO: Well, yeah. That's why when I tore the light off of the cop car, I handed it to Zod like a child gives a gift to a parent. Terence, Sarah and I – we had a great synergy between us.

GB: Were you very conscious of Donner's concept of verisimilitude during the making of the two films?
JO: Well, it was an attitude that I thought was great. It's the reason why the Donner cut of *Superman II* is so much better than Lester's cut. Lester put comedy in it and Donner

didn't. The Donner cut was more serious; the Lester cut was almost too cartoonish and unbelievable. You've got one director who is a serious movie director and the other guy who is a television director. It's like night and day. Donner is a brilliant director. Richard Lester was an excuse for a director.

GB: You helped Christopher Reeve to prepare physically for the part of Superman. Were you training him alongside Dave Prowse?[32]
JO: No. When they first brought Christopher over for his screen test, he was 170 lbs. And he had an ego. He didn't want to put a shield underneath his costume to create the illusion of ripples and muscles and everything. David Prowse was a weightlifter and a bodybuilder, but bulk, you understand? I said to him, 'As thin as he is, Christopher has the frame to put muscle on, so do it like Steve Reeves.' Steve Reeves played Hercules. He was a bodybuilder – he was Mr World, Mr Universe. He was one of the first bodybuilders that never used bulk; he used definition. He won all the big awards because he only weighed 196 lbs. He wasn't like Arnold Schwarzenegger, who was overbuilt. And then when Steve Reeves did movies, they put weight on him to make him look like Hercules, this big-muscled strong man. I said to David, 'That's all you need to do with Christopher; you don't need to spend all this time with him pumping iron. You need to build him with definition' – because it takes less time to do that. You can achieve that quicker than you can from someone stuffing food in their mouth, building and adding weight. And it would look better on film, because when you shoot something with the camera it automatically looks bigger. The camera makes you look bigger than you are. Christopher eventually had the right definition, and it looked brilliant. He looked like he was actually that rippled. It wasn't overdone.

GB: You knew Tom Mankiewicz very well, and would be directed by him in Dragnet...
JO: Yeah, he was like the right hand of Donner. Tom was around a lot during the filming of *Superman* because he was a contributor with Donner, and Mankiewicz's father was the big man in the industry. Tom was a very creative, very smart guy. Nobody's fool. And he and Donner were really good friends. They were both Superman fanatics. If the Salkinds would have let Donner finish *Superman II*, he would have done *Superman III* and *Superman IV*, and the Superman franchise would have been 100 per cent different. It would have just been a much better franchise; they'd still be doing them correctly.

GB: In his autobiography, Mankiewicz (2015: 209) mentions a lively encounter that you had with the Superman producers.
JO: We had been working in London for about eight weeks. As you know, it gets a little dismal in London. It was raining, the sun wasn't shining. And we had a few days off. I thought to myself, 'I'm going to fly back to L.A. for a couple of days. I'm going to jump on a plane.' Well, you're not supposed to do that unless you get clearance. If you're a

principal actor in the picture, God forbid something happens to you and the production is screwed. But I just did it: I jumped on a plane and I flew home to Beverly Hills. There were no cellphones in those days, so when I got back to Beverly Hills I picked up a payphone, called my accountant, and said, 'I'm home, and I've got to do a few things while I'm here. We should have a lot of money in the bank.' She said, 'Jack, we have a lot of *paper* in the bank.' I said, 'What are you talking about?' She said, 'We have a lot of cheques that haven't cleared.' I said, 'How could that be? I've been working for eight weeks.' So then she explained it to me: the Salkinds had written what you call a non-descript cheque, which meant that the cheques had to go back to the bank in Switzerland, and they hadn't cleared them for payment. I said, 'What the fuck?' So, standing in the same payphone booth, I made a collect call to Pierre Spengler's office. He gets on the phone, and he says, 'My God, where are you?' I said, 'I'm in California.' He said, 'But you've got to go to work on Monday.' And I said, 'Here's my problem: my doctor says I've got this crick in my back, and I'm probably going to have to lay out in the sun for a while until some money gets into my bank account.' He said, 'What are you talking about?' I said, 'Well, I've got a bunch of paper in my bank but no money. I've been working every day, how come there is no money in my bank?' 'Call me back in fifteen minutes.' So I said, 'Okay' and a little later I called him back. He said, 'Everything is taken care of. Now, you've got to be here for Monday for work.' I called my accountant, and within two hours' time, money had appeared in my bank. So I took a flight on Sunday at midnight and got into Heathrow at seven on Monday morning. I walked into Pinewood direct from Heathrow, and I walked right upstairs to Pierre Spengler's office. Pierre was just coming back from France; he had needed to go there to explain to Alexander Salkind why he had sent this money to America. He came into his office, and he said to me: 'What kind of bullshit is this?' And I reached over, pulled him across the desk, looked at him and said, 'Let me say something to you, man. You screw with my paycheque one more time, I promise you I will drop you in the Hudson with a camera in your fucking hands.' And I dropped him back in his seat. He said, 'You're threatening me.' I said, 'Uh-uh. You got it all wrong. I'm promising you. This bullshit stops here. You should be paying me the way you're supposed to pay me.' Well, I was the only one who never had a problem with their paycheque after that. I never had another problem with the producers. Pierre's a nice guy, but they all robbed a lot of money on the movie.

But the Salkinds were notorious. We started shooting the picture at the Shepperton studio. Now, the Salkinds knew they were eventually going to move the production over to Pinewood. Pinewood didn't have enough room at first, so the Salkinds went to Shepperton, cleaned up some space, threw a little furniture around, and it appeared that we were going to be shooting *Superman* at Shepperton. Well, they had to get Brando on camera during the first eleven days of shooting. They needed to get him on film, so that they could go to the bank, show the footage and get money. So they hired this crew to go and shoot Brando's scenes, and everybody on the crew thinks, 'Wow, we're on the

Superman movie, this is going to be a year's work. We'll be around for a while.' Here's what the Salkinds did: we worked at Shepperton for a month or so, and then we moved over to Pinewood. Well, Pinewood has a house crew. So all these guys that were working at Shepperton got fired. That was just the kind of bullshit [the Salkinds] did.

GB: What are your memories of Marlon Brando?
JO: Brando was just brilliant. When he came on the set you could hear a pin drop. He commanded that kind of respect. And he *gave* that kind of respect, too. When Brando came to work in the morning, he'd say hello to everybody. 'Hello, how are you doing? How is your family?' It was like a family kind of deal. Brando worked nine to five, and at five o'clock when it was time to go home – boom – 'See ya,' and he'd be gone. What are you going to do, argue with Marlon Brando? I don't think so.

GB: While at Pinewood, you shot scenes for Superman II *with Gene Hackman, with whom you had previously worked on* March or Die. *How would you describe Hackman's approach to acting?*
JO: Hackman is a mechanical actor. He was very technical. He had his eyelines all set up and everything; and he didn't want the director to position him there and move him around like a doll. He hated it if the director hadn't done their homework as to how they wanted to set up a shot. I'll give you a good example from *March or Die*. Dick Richards was not the greatest director in the world. He was a nice guy but he was a television director; he did commercials and stuff. Dick Richards was so fucking indecisive. We went on the set one day, and Richards starts moving the actors around when he gets them on the set. Hackman said to him, 'Stop right there. Here's the deal: you go home and do your homework, and when you've figured out what you want to do, call me up. But if you think you're going to move me around like a puppet because you haven't done your homework, this ain't going to work. I can't work that way.' And he walked off the set. You learn from people like that. Hackman's a brilliant actor. He told me that they threw him out of most of the acting schools when he was starting out.

GB: On the set of Superman, *how would you spend the time in between takes?*
JO: We did a lot of laughing. We did a lot of practical jokes. It was a very relaxed atmosphere. Sarah [Douglas] was terrific; she's just brilliant. Margot [Kidder] was nuttier than shit. Maggie was a well-established star, and she was nuts. Everybody knew she was nuts. You just had a lot of laughs with her. And Valerie Perrine is out to lunch all the time. So we had a lot of fun. Terence [Stamp] was so serious. Terence had changed his whole life. He was a wild man when he was younger. But then he had gone to India and cleaned himself up. When he came back, *Superman* was the first movie he did in this new persona. Terence was a professional, boy. We all helped each other. We all spent time together off camera; it was like a family affair.

GB: Would you watch the dailies during production?
JO: I never watched dailies. There was only one time that I went in to watch any footage. We were shooting *Superman II* longer than we should have, and we all had to stop and go back to shooting the first movie. That's why there was so much footage of *Superman II* done by Donner. They had to go back and finish the first movie, because they had to deliver the picture by a certain date. So Alexander Salkind, of course, was looking to hold Warner Brothers up for more money. And Warners said, 'If you don't deliver this picture we're going to fine you.' Alexander said, 'Hold it. Are you telling me that you're relieving me of my distribution contract? That I can bring other distributors in to look at the picture? Is that what you're telling me?' So Warner Brothers got very insulted, and said, 'Yeah, take it that way.' So he did. He arranged a screening and he brought all these people in to watch the fight scene from *Superman II*. He screened the fight scene, and Warner Brothers couldn't get the bands off the money fast enough. Let me tell you something: when they saw that fight scene, everybody wanted the picture. Warner Brothers shit themselves. Salkind owned them right there. And that's the way he was. There was so much conniving, and it was so sad because they had such a great product, man. God, they had a great product.

GB: Apparently, the original plan was for the three Kryptonian villains to return in **Superman III.**
JO: That's right. Yeah. We all believed that. At the end of *Superman II*, we got locked up and taken off to jail. But that scene was cut from the film. It all changed when Lester came on board. *Superman III* is his baby and look what he did. Look at the difference between *Superman II*, *III*, and *IV*. They got progressively worse. The Salkinds sold the franchise to Cannon. And Christopher wrote the script for *Superman IV*.[33] How could you degrade yourself like that? Christopher didn't give a fuck, because they paid him a lot of money. It's sad, because it shows you how much he cared about his art. If Christopher Reeve would have stood up on *Superman II* and said, 'You know what, if Donner doesn't come back, neither do I,' they would have had no alternative but to bring Donner back. Hackman never went back to work. And I almost didn't go back. The producers were fools, because how do you cut Marlon Brando out of a picture? They just didn't want to pay him the points. In the Donner cut, you've got twenty-six minutes of Brando in there, and it makes the movie a lot better. So the producers did things that hurt the franchise, which meant they didn't give a shit about the public. And they were notorious for that. I love the Donner cut. It's sad that Donner wasn't able to finish it the way he wanted to. He had to use screen tests for some of the fill-ins, you know? He was such a brilliant director. He was so creative and he was so into Superman. He lived it, boy, he was really into it.

GB: It has been 40 years since the release of **Superman: The Movie** *and the production of* **Superman II.** *How do you regard the two films today?*
JO: They worked out so well. The [aerial] fights with Christopher over the city were technically done very, very well. It wasn't a bunch of blue-screen shit. Here it is 40 years later and it's still as popular as it was the day we did it. I can look at *Superman* today and say, 'Show me a picture better than this' – I mean, technology-wise. And even acting-wise. You're never going to get another Christopher. He could be the biggest asshole in the world but he was great as Clark Kent and Superman. He worked both roles very well. And Margot was a great Lois Lane; no-one else has matched her. The villains haven't been matched. Kevin Spacey is a great actor but he's no Gene Hackman.[34] And Ned Beatty is a trippy guy; he was wonderful as Hackman's fumbling assistant. It was a pleasure to be able to do a role that gave me as much satisfaction as it gave the audience. And I had a director that let me go do it. That's what makes Donner a great director. He allowed me to pursue that character. Actually, I'm thinking of going and getting the rights to do a Superman movie and bring Christopher back.

GB: How would you do that?
JO: Well, the technology is there.

GB: The way that certain actors have been resurrected in recent **Star Wars** *movies?*
JO: Yeah, the holograms are there. I could bring Christopher back, I could bring Brando back, I could make the villains any age I want, and we have the voices of the three of us. It would not be difficult at all. We're very seriously contemplating that, and I think we're going to do it. The picture would be huge. Imagine bringing Christopher back on screen, and going back to the original costume. They've gotten so dark with the character in the recent Superman movies. We could take it back to the all-American way. I've got a couple of storylines that I think would fly like an eagle. And the fans would go nuts. I think it would be unbelievable.

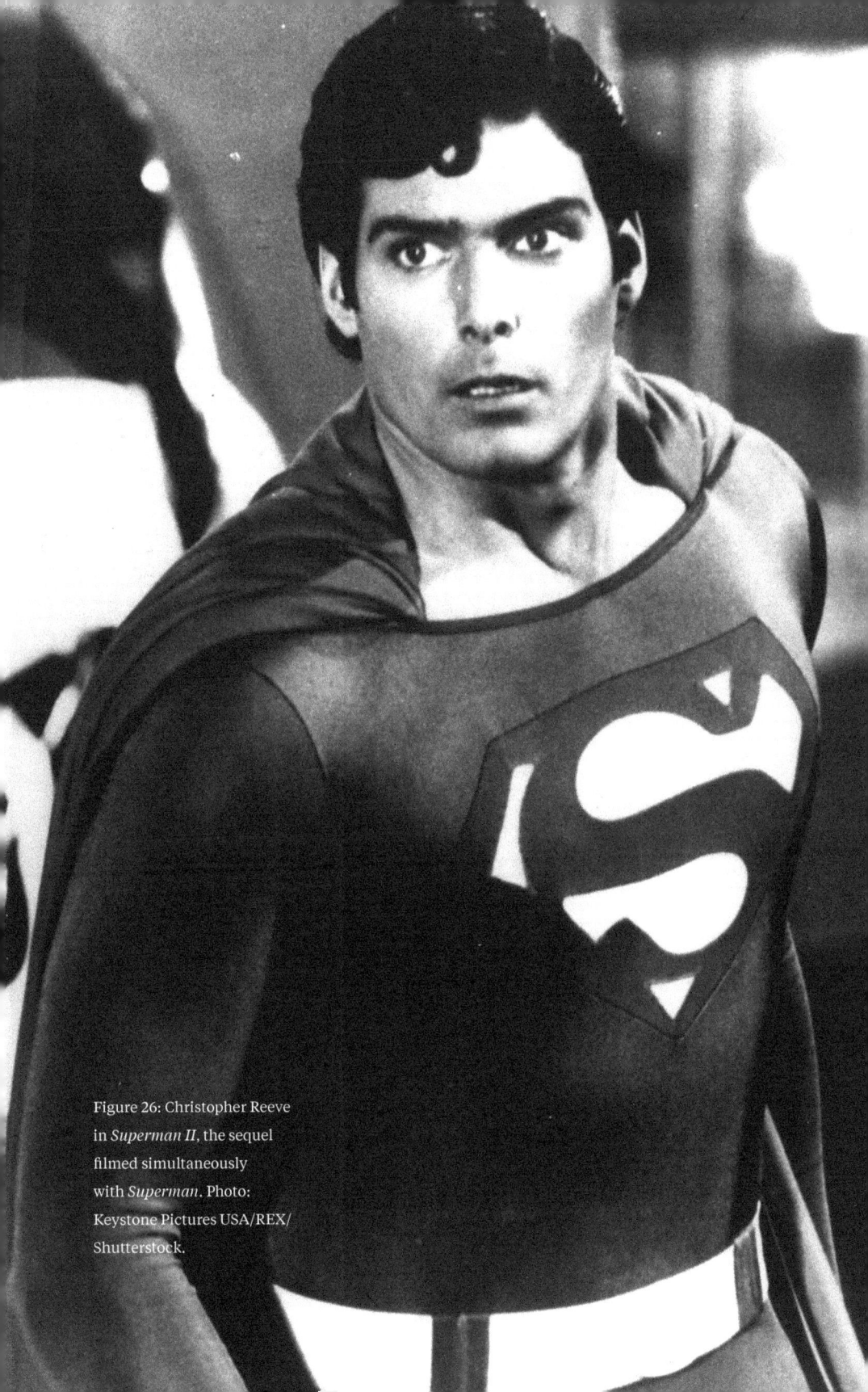

Figure 26: Christopher Reeve in *Superman II*, the sequel filmed simultaneously with *Superman*. Photo: Keystone Pictures USA/REX/Shutterstock.

NOTES

1. The interviews in this book were conducted between January 2017 and January 2018.
2. This was not David Newman and Robert Benton's first encounter with Superman. In 1966, they wrote the book of the Broadway musical *It's a Bird…It's a Plane…It's Superman* (a catchphrase, incidentally, never spoken in *Superman: The Movie*).
3. Brando's career renaissance in the 1970s culminated in Academy Award recognition for *The Godfather* and a further nomination for *Last Tango in Paris* (1972); Hackman won a Best Actor Oscar for *The French Connection* (1971).
4. Reportedly, Brando's contract also entitled him to 11.3 per cent of the domestic gross and 5.6 per cent of the foreign gross (see Harmetz 1981). According to *Newsweek*, the actor filed lawsuits against *Superman*'s producers and Warner Brothers 'for doing him out of his share of gross receipts' (Kroll 1979: 51).
5. Kirk Alyn portrayed the eponymous hero in the movie serials *Superman* (1948) and *Atom Man vs. Superman* (1950), both of which featured Noel Neill as Lois Lane. Neill reprised her role in five seasons of the television series *Adventures of Superman*, from 1953 to 1958.
6. Spengler is likely referring to *Superman and the Mole Men* (1951), starring George Reeves as the eponymous hero and Phyllis Coates as Lois Lane. This feature-length film would subsequently be condensed into a two-part episode of the television series, *Adventures of Superman*.
7. Donner filmed the diner scene in which Clark Kent, sans-super powers, is viciously assaulted by a loutish redneck. He also shot *Superman II*'s coda, depicting the thug's comeuppance.
8. In October 2017, Warner Brothers released an extended, 188-minute television edit of *Superman: The Movie* on Blu-ray.
9. Spielberg served as the executive producer of Donner's box-office triumph, *The Goonies* (1985).
10. In the draft screenplay signed by Puzo, Benton and the Newmans in 1976, Superman mistakes the 'shining bald head' of Telly Savalas for that of Lex Luthor. According to the screenplay, Superman 'swoops down on his prey', prompting Savalas – 'with lollipop and big grin' – to remark: 'Hey! Superman! Who loves ya, baby?'
11. In Lester's theatrical version of *Superman II*, Lara (Susannah York) tells her Kryptonian son: 'If you intend to live your life with a mortal, you must live as a mortal. You must become one of them.'

Superman subsequently relinquishes his powers so as to consummate a romantic relationship with Lois Lane.
12. Salkind is referring to the opening title sequence of *Superman III*, a slapstick tour-de-force unlike any sequence in the franchise's previous instalments.
13. Twentieth Century Fox released *Batman: The Movie* – directed by Leslie H. Martinson, and starring Adam West and Burt Ward as the dynamic duo – in July 1966.
14. Mankiewicz's directorial credits include the Hollywood comedies *Dragnet* (1987) and *Delirious* (1991).
15. Mankiewicz died on 31 July 2010.
16. Donner directed all four films in the *Lethal Weapon* franchise (1987–98).
17. The story that Kidder refers to is entitled 'The Private Life of Clark Kent: Right Down My Alley', published in *Superman*, v.37 n.289 (July 1975), and written by E. Nelson Bridwell with artwork by Curt Swan.
18. Tom Mankiewicz was the son of esteemed Hollywood filmmaker Joseph L. Mankiewicz, whose directing credits include *The Ghost and Mrs. Muir* (1947), *A Letter to Three Wives* (1949), *All About Eve* (1950), *The Quiet American* (1958), *Cleopatra* (1963) and *Sleuth* (1972). Among the writing credits of Tom Mankiewicz's uncle, Herman J. Mankiewicz, is Orson Welles' *Citizen Kane* (1941).
19. Posing as newlyweds, Clark and Lois undertake an assignment at Niagara Falls. When Clark tries to retrieve his eyeglasses from a roaring fireplace, Lois inspects his hand for signs of injury, ultimately realizing that he is Superman.
20. Kidder's vociferous criticism of the *Superman* producers was printed in Pirie (1981).
21. Jack Larson played Jimmy Olsen in all six seasons of the television series, *Adventures of Superman* (1952–58).
22. Originally cast as Perry White, Keenan Wynn suffered a heart attack on the eve of production. He was replaced at the eleventh hour by former child star Jackie Cooper.
23. Johns served as an intern for Donner before launching his writing career at DC Comics. The pair has collaborated on Superman comic-book stories including 'Last Son' (2006–8) and 'Escape from Bizarro World' (2007).
24. The supporting cast of CW's *Supergirl* (2015–date) includes *Superman* alumni Sarah Douglas (*Superman: The Movie*; *Superman II*; *Superman II: The Richard Donner Cut*), Helen Slater (*Supergirl*, 1984), and Dean Cain and Teri Hatcher (*Lois & Clark: The New Adventures of Superman*, 1993–97).
25. Prior to *Superman: The Movie*, East portrayed Huckleberry Finn in two films for United Artists: *Tom Sawyer* (1973) and *Huckleberry Finn* (1974).
26. Like *Superman*, much of *Star Wars* was shot in England (in this case, Elstree Studios) with a largely British production crew.
27. East's entire vocal performance was dubbed by Reeve in post-production.
28. The Christopher & Dana Reeve Foundation is 'dedicated to advancing quality of life and discovering cures for spinal cord injury'. https://www.christopherreeve.org/
29. Larry Hagman features in a cameo role as a libidinous army major.

30. Terence Stamp's hiatus from western cinema came to an end with *Superman: The Movie*.
31. Among Non's infantile traits is an effort to master his nascent powers and an attraction to colourful objects (such as the flashing siren of a police car).
32. For the role of Superman, Reeve embarked on a rigorous fitness regime under the aegis of actor and bodybuilder David Prowse, who played Darth Vadar in the original *Star Wars* trilogy (1977–83).
33. Reeve is officially credited only with devising the story of *Superman IV* along with Lawrence Konner and Mark Rosenthal, both of whom share credit for the film's screenplay.
34. Spacey played Lex Luthor in Bryan Singer's *Superman Returns* (2006).

REFERENCES

Bettinson, Gary (2018), 'Tales from the Kryptonians: *Superman: The Movie* at 40,' *Cinema Retro*, n. 42, September.

Biskind, Peter (1998), *Easy Riders, Raging Bulls: How the Sex 'N' Drugs 'N' Rock 'N' Roll Generation Saved Hollywood*, London: Bloomsbury.

Bridwell, E. Nelson (1975), 'The Private Life of Clark Kent: Right Down My Alley', *Superman*, v.37 n.289, July, New York: DC Comics.

Carroll, Noël (1998), *Interpreting the Moving Image*, Cambridge, UK: Cambridge University Press.

Harmetz, Aljean (1981), 'The life and exceedingly hard times of Superman', *The New York Times*, 14 June, http://www.nytimes.com/1981/06/14/movies/the-life-and-exceedingly-hard-times-of-superman.html?pagewanted=all. Accessed 3 February 2018.

Itzkoff, Dave (2017), 'New selections for National Film Registry include "Superman", "Titanic" and "Spartacus"', *The New York Times*, 13 December , https://www.nytimes.com/2017/12/13/movies/national-film-registry-superman-titanic-spartacus-die-hard.html. Accessed 11 February 2018.

Johns, Geoff and Donner, Richard (2007), 'Escape from Bizarro World', *Action Comics*, n. 856-857, New York: DC Comics.

Johns, Geoff and Donner, Richard (2006-8), 'Last Son', *Action Comics*, n. 844-846, 851, Annual 11, New York: DC Comics.

Klinger, Judson (1981), 'The education of Margot Kidder', *Rolling Stone*, n. 347, 9 July, pp. 21–23, 76, 79.

Kroll, Jack (1979), 'Superman to the rescue!', *Newsweek*, XCIII:1, 1 January.

Mankiewicz, Tom and Crane, Robert (2015), *My Life as a Mankiewicz: An Insider's Journey Through Hollywood*, Lexington, KY: The University Press of Kentucky.

Pirie, Dave (1981), 'The truth about Superman', *Time Out*, n. 573, 10–16 April, pp. 18–20.

Reeve, Christopher (1999), *Still Me*, London: Arrow Books.

FILMS CITED

2001: A Space Odyssey (Stanley Kubrick, 1968)
All About Eve (Joseph L. Mankiewicz, 1950)
The Amityville Horror (Stuart Rosenberg, 1979)
Apollo 13 (Ron Howard, 1995)
Atom Man vs. Superman (Spencer Gordon Bennet, 1950)
Avengers Assemble (Joss Whedon, 2012)
Back to the Future (Robert Zemeckis, 1985)
Batman: The Movie (Leslie H. Martinson, 1966)
Batman v. Superman: Dawn of Justice (Zack Snyder, 2016)
Blue (Silvio Narizzano, 1968)
Blue Champagne (Blaine Novak, 1992)
Bonnie and Clyde (Arthur Penn, 1967)
The Bostonians (James Ivory, 1984)
Cabaret (Bob Fosse, 1972)
Citizen Kane (Orson Welles, 1941)
Cleopatra (Joseph L. Mankiewicz, 1963)
Deathtrap (Sidney Lumet, 1982)
Delirious (Tom Mankiewicz, 1991)
Dragnet (Tom Mankiewicz, 1987)
Duel (Steven Spielberg, 1971)
Far from the Madding Crowd (John Schlesinger, 1967)
Farewell, My Lovely (Dick Richards, 1975)
Fiddler on the Roof (Norman Jewison, 1971)
The Four Musketeers (Richard Lester, 1974)
The French Connection (William Friedkin, 1971)
The Ghost and Mrs. Muir (Joseph L. Mankiewicz, 1947)
The Godfather (Francis Ford Coppola, 1972)
Goldfinger (Guy Hamilton, 1964)
The Goonies (Richard Donner, 1985)
Gray Lady Down (David Greene, 1978)
A Hard Day's Night (Richard Lester, 1964)
The Hazing (Douglas Curtis, 1977)

Huckleberry Finn (J. Lee Thompson, 1974)
In the Gloaming (Christopher Reeve, 1997)
Iron Man (Jon Favreau, 2008)
Jaws (Steven Spielberg, 1975)
Justice League (Zack Snyder, 2017)
King Kong (John Guillermin, 1976)
Last Tango in Paris (Bernardo Bertolucci, 1972)
Lethal Weapon (Richard Donner, 1987)
A Letter to Three Wives (Joseph L. Mankiewicz, 1949)
March or Die (Dick Richards, 1977)
The Missouri Breaks (Arthur Penn, 1976)
Monsignor (Frank Perry, 1982)
Mutiny on the Bounty (Lewis Milestone, 1962)
Noises Off… (Peter Bogdanovich, 1992)
The Omen (Richard Donner, 1976)
The People That Time Forgot (Kevin Connor, 1977)
Pride of Lions (Sidney J. Furie, 2014)
The Quiet American (Joseph L. Mankiewicz, 1958)
Ready Player One (Steven Spielberg, 2018)
The Remains of the Day (James Ivory, 1993)
Sleuth (Joseph L. Mankiewicz, 1972)
Somewhere in Time (Jeannot Szwarc, 1980)
Star Wars: Episode IV – A New Hope (George Lucas, 1977)
Street Smart (Jerry Schatzberg, 1987)
The Sugarland Express (Steven Spielberg, 1974)
Supergirl (Jeannot Szwarc, 1984)
Superman (Spencer Gordon Bennet, Thomas Carr, 1948)
Superman II (Richard Lester, 1980)
Superman II: The Richard Donner Cut (Richard Donner, 2006)
Superman III (Richard Lester, 1983)
Superman IV: The Quest for Peace (Sidney J. Furie, 1987)
Superman and the Mole Men (Lee Sholem, 1951)
Superman Returns (Bryan Singer, 2006)
Superman: The Movie (Richard Donner, 1978)
Switching Channels (Ted Kotcheff, 1988)
The Three Musketeers (Richard Lester, 1973)
Tom Sawyer (Don Taylor, 1973)
Wonder Woman (Patty Jenkins, 2017)

Lightning Source UK Ltd.
Milton Keynes UK
UKHW051111060223
416527UK00012B/579